Zaner-Bloser
Handwriting
With a new alphabet

Author

Clinton S. Hackney

Contributing Authors

Pamela J. Farris
Janice T. Jones
Linda Leonard Lamme

Zaner-Bloser, Inc., P.O. Box 16764, Columbus, Ohio 43216-6764   1-800-421-3018

Copyright © 1996 Zaner-Bloser, Inc.   ISBN 0-88085-726-9

Developed by Kirchoff/Wohlberg, Inc., in cooperation with Zaner-Bloser Publishers

Printed in the United States of America

96 97 98 99 WC 5 4 3 2

You already know handwriting is important.
Now take a look at...

NEW
Zaner-Bloser Handwriting

Easier to read!　Easier to write!　Easier to teach!

I see Zaner-Bloser's alphabet in the books I read.

I like Zaner-Bloser because it's so easy to write.

Zaner-Bloser's new program is easy to teach.

You already know handwriting is important, but did you know...

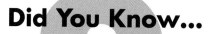

Did You Know...

Annually, the U.S. Postal Service receives 38 million illegibly addressed letters, costing American taxpayers $4 million each year.

—American Demographics, Dec. 1992

Did You Know...

Hundreds of thousands of tax returns are delayed every year because figures, notes, and signatures are illegible.

—Better Handwriting in 30 Days, 1989

Did You Know...

Poor handwriting costs American business $200 million annually.

—American Demographics, Dec. 1992

Zaner-Bloser's CONTINUOUS-STROKE manuscript alphabet

Aa Bb Cc Dd Ee Ff Gg
Oo Pp Qq Rr Ss Tt

Easier to Read

Our vertical manuscript alphabet is like the alphabet kids see every day inside and outside of the classroom. They see it in their school books, in important environmental print like road signs, and in books and cartoons they read for fun.

"[Slanted] manuscript is not only harder to learn than traditional [vertical] print, but it creates substantially more letter recognition errors and causes more letter confusion than does the traditional style."

–Debby Kuhl and Peter Dewitz in a paper presented at the 1994 meeting of the American Educational Research Association

CALIFORNIA LIN 216

STOP

Vertical manuscript is the alphabet we see every day.

Hh Ii Jj Kk Ll Mm Nn
Uu Vv Ww Xx Yy Zz

Easier to Write

Our vertical manuscript alphabet is written with continuous strokes—fewer pencil lifts—so there's a greater sense of flow in writing. And kids can write every letter once they learn four simple strokes that even kindergartners can manage.

Four simple strokes: circle, horizontal line, vertical line, slanted line

"The writing hand has to change direction more often when writing the [slanted] alphabet, do more retracing of lines, and make more strokes that occur later in children's development."

–Steve Graham in *Focus on Exceptional Children*, 1992

Many kids can already write their names when they start school (vertical manuscript).

Kirk

Why should they have to relearn them in another form (slanted manuscript)? With Zaner-Bloser, they don't have to.

Kirk

Easier to Teach

Our vertical manuscript alphabet is easy to teach because there's no reteaching involved. Children are already familiar with our letterforms—they've seen them in their environment and they've learned them at home.

"Before starting school, many children learn how to write traditional [vertical] manuscript letters from their parents or preschool teachers. Learning a special alphabet such as [slanted] means that these children will have to relearn many of the letters they can already write."

–Steve Graham in *Focus on Exceptional Children*, 1992

Zaner-Bloser's NEW SIMPLIFIED cursive alphabet

Aa Bb Cc Dd Ee Ff Gg

Nn Oo Pp Qq Rr Ss

Simplified letterforms... Easier to read and write

old letterform

Letterforms are simplified so they're easier to write and easier to identify in writing. The new simplified **Q** now looks like a **Q** instead of a number 2.

old letterform

Our simplified letterforms use the headline, midline, and baseline as a guide for where letters start and stop. The new simplified **d** touches the headline instead of stopping halfway.

old letterform

No more "cane stems!" Our new simplified letterforms begin with a small curve instead of fancy loops that can be difficult for students to write.

vi

Hh Ii Jj Kk Ll Mm
Tt Uu Vv Ww Xx Yy Zz

Simplified letterforms...
Easier to teach

When handwriting is easy for students to write, instruction time is cut way back! That's the teaching advantage with Zaner-Bloser Handwriting. Our cursive letterforms are simplified so instead of spending a lot of time teaching fancy loops that give kids trouble, teachers give instruction for simple, basic handwriting that students can use for the rest of their lives.

And remember, with Zaner-Bloser Handwriting, students learn to write manuscript with continuous strokes. That means that when it's time for those students to begin writing cursive, the transition comes naturally because they already know the flow of continuous strokes.

These simple letters are so much easier to teach!

The Student Edition...set up for student success

Uppercase and lowercase letterforms are taught together.

Students master manuscript writing before they begin to write cursive.

Students trace models first before writing on their own.

Writing practice is done directly beneath a model that is easy for both right- and left-handers to see.

g G   j J   q Q

Trace and write the letters.

g g g g g g   G G G G G

j j j j j j   J J J J J

q q q q q q   Q Q Q Q Q

My Own Words

Circle your best letters.

26

Grade 2C Student Edition

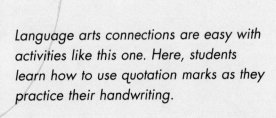

Language arts connections are easy with activities like this one. Here, students learn how to use quotation marks as they practice their handwriting.

Write titles of songs. Use quotation marks— " and ".

"Six Little Ducks"

"When You Wish Upon a Star"

"Under the Sea"   "Sing"

On Your Own Write the title of a song you like to sing.

31

Grade 2C Student Edition

Manuscript and cursive writing helps children become comfortable with reading both forms of writing.

Letter models with arrows show stroke direction and sequence.

Students first practice letters, then joinings, and finally complete words.

Students evaluate their own handwriting on every page.

Circle j and *j* in these words.

joeys juggling jars
joeys juggling jars

Trace and write.

Join *j* and other letters.

Write words with *j*.

Circle your best *j*.

62

Grade 2C Student Edition

Activities like this one, in which students write the names of different cities, offer teachers the opportunity to bring multiculturalism into the classroom.

Begin each name with an uppercase letter.

Write names of cities.

Oakland   Akron   Dallas

Atlanta   Orlando   Detroit

On Your Own
Write the name of the town or city and the state where you live.

Circle the name you wrote best.

23

Grade 2C Student Edition

At-a-glance stroke descriptions are short and easy to find.

Fun activities and language arts connections reinforce many different skills.

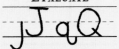
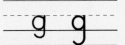

CONTINUOUS STROKE

Touch below the midline; circle back (left) all the way around. Push up straight to the midline. Pull down straight through the baseline; curve back (left).

Touch the midline; pull down straight through the baseline; curve back (left). Lift. Dot.

Touch below the midline; circle back (left) all the way around. Push up straight to the midline. Pull down straight through the baseline; curve forward (right).

FuN and Games

Charades
Write a noun that begins with **g**, **j**, or **q** on each of twelve index cards. Have each student choose a word and act it out until a classmate guesses it and writes it on the board. (visual)

26

Trace and write the letters.

g g g g g g   G G G G G

j j j j j j   J J J J J

q q q q q q   Q Q Q Q Q

My Own Words

Circle your best letters.

26

MODEL THE WRITING
Write **g, j,** and **q** on guidelines as you say the stroke descriptions for each letter. Invite several students to dip a small sponge in water and use it to write these letters on the chalkboard while others say the descriptions with you. Follow the same procedure for **G, J,** and **Q**.

A CLOSER LOOK
Call attention to the size and shape of the letters by asking questions such as these:
Which letters are tall?
Which letters go below the baseline?
Which letters have a backward circle?
Which letters begin with a pull down straight stroke?
Which letter has a slide left stroke?

PRACTICE
Let students practice writing the letter pairs **gG, jJ,** and **qQ** on laminated writing cards or slates before they write on the pages.

EVALUATE

To help students evaluate their writing, ask questions such as these:
Is the backward circle of your **g** round?
Does the slide left stroke of your **G** touch the midline?
Did you remember to dot your **j**?
Is your **J** straight up and down?
Does your **q** touch the next headline?
Does your **Q** look like an **O** except for the slant right stroke?

BETTER LETTERS

Remind students that descenders should fill the space below the baseline and touch the next headline.

Grade 2C Teacher Edition

Brief teaching notes save you valuable time.

A Better Letters section provides helpful reminders.

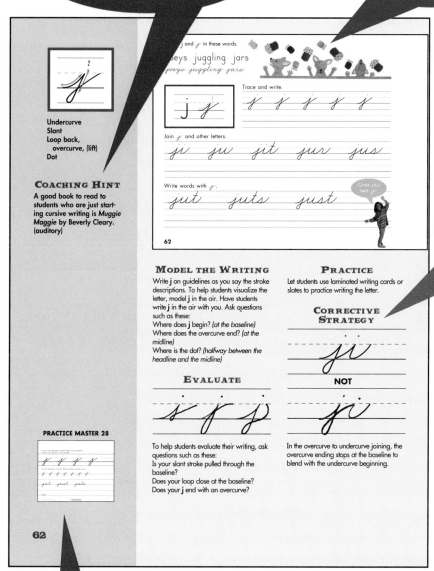

Coaching Hints offer insight and additional information.

The student page is close to the instruction for that page.

Corrective Strategies offer solutions to common handwriting problems.

Visual references to practice masters for each lesson save you time.

Grade 2C Teacher Edition

Grade 2C Practice Masters

An accompanying book of practice masters offers additional practice for every letter and skill students learn. It also includes resources to make teaching easier—certificates, an evaluation record, letters to send home to keep parents and guardians involved, and Spanish activities.

Evaluation and Assessment... consistent guidance throughout the year

Student self-evaluation...

In every lesson. Students evaluate their own handwriting and circle their best work.

In every review. Twelve times during the year, students review the letterforms and joinings they've learned and again evaluate their handwriting.

Teacher assessment...

In every lesson and review. As students evaluate their own writing, teachers can assess their letterforms, as well as their comprehension of good handwriting. Corrective Strategies for each lesson offer teachers helpful hints for common handwriting problems.

Through relevant practice activities. Students' work in relevant practice activities offers lots of opportunity for informal assessment of handwriting, language arts, and other areas.

The Keys to Legibility

These four Keys to Legibility are taught and reviewed throughout the program.
They remind students that their goal should be legible handwriting.

Size

Consistently sized letters are easy to read. Students learn to use midlines and headlines to guide the size of their letters.

Slant

Letters with a consistent slant are easy to read. Students learn how to position their papers and hold their pencils so consistent slant comes with ease.

Shape

Four simple strokes—undercurve, downcurve, overcurve, and slant—make it easy for students to write letters with consistent and proper shape.

Spacing

Correct spacing between letters and words makes handwriting easy to read. Practical hints show students how to determine correct spacing.

Review

Remember! $\mathcal{J}$ is joined to the letter that follows. $\mathcal{T}$, $\mathcal{F}$, $\mathcal{I}$, and $\mathcal{Q}$ are not joined.

Throughout the program, students evaluate their own handwriting and circle their best work.

Write names of kings and queens.

Frederick   Theresa

(Frederick)   Theresa

John   Isabella

John   Isabella

Circle your best word.

Write this sentence.

I saw Queen Tzu.

I (saw) Queen Tzu.

Circle the word with the best size and shape.

112

Completed Grade 2C Student Edition

ee   four

ee   four

five   six   seven

five   six   seven

eight   nine   ten

eight   nine   ten

Write the answers in words.

one plus two   three

eight minus two   six

four plus three   (seven)

Circle your best number word.

123

Relevant practice activities allow the teacher to informally assess handwriting and other skills, such as math.

A huge collection of supplementary materials... makes handwriting even easier to teach!

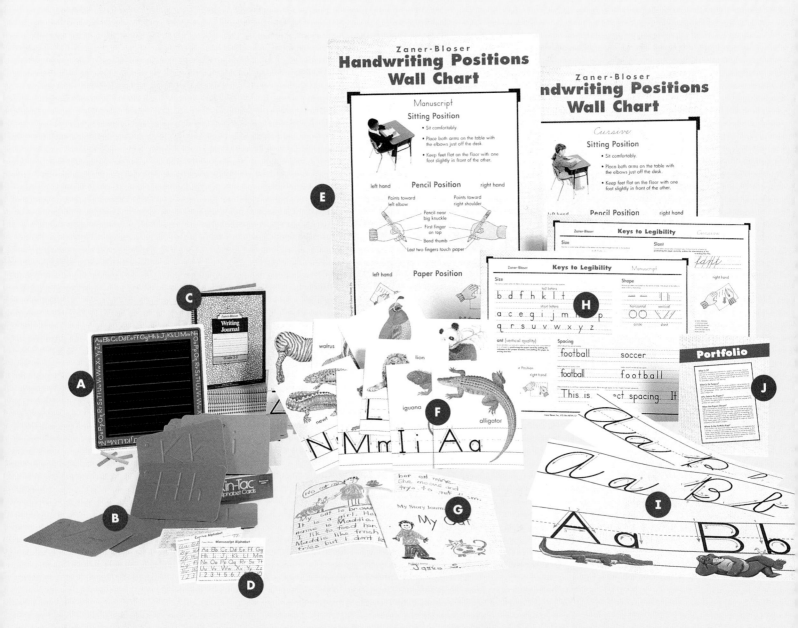

For more information about these materials, call 1-800-421-3018.

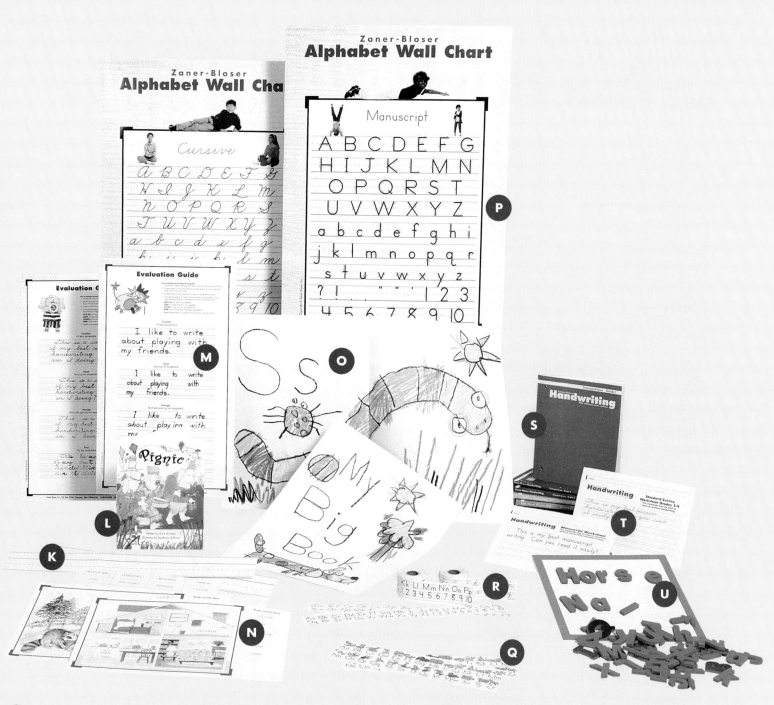

K   **Blank Sentence Strips** *grades K–6*

L   **Pignic Alphabet Book** *grades K–2*

M   **Evaluation Guides** *grades 1–6*

N   **Vinyl Storyboard Set** *grades K–2*

O   **Make-Your-Own Big Book** *grades K–2*

P   **Alphabet Wall Chart** *grades K–4*

Q   **Illustrated Alphabet Strips** *grades K–2*

R   **Desk Strips** *grades 1–6*

S   **Book of Transparencies** *grades 1–6*

T   **Parent/Student Worksheets** *grades 2–6*

U   **Write-On, Wipe-Off Magnetic Board With Letters** *grades K–2*

Vertical vs. *Slanted Manuscript*

What the research shows

Using a slanted alphabet has been a trend in handwriting instruction. It's actually not a new development—the first slanted alphabet was created in 1968. A sort of bridge between manuscript and cursive, this slanted alphabet used unconnected letter-forms like the traditional vertical manuscript, but its letterforms were slanted like cursive.

It seemed like a good idea. This alphabet was to be easier to write than cursive, yet similar enough to cursive that children wouldn't learn two *completely* different alphabets. But after several years of use in some schools, research has uncovered some unfortunate findings.

Slanted manuscript can be difficult to write

Slanted manuscript was created to be similar to cursive, so it uses more complicated strokes such as small curves, and these strokes can be difficult for young children.

Vertical manuscript, on the other hand, is consistent with the development of young children. Each of its letters is formed with simple strokes—straight lines, circles, and slanted lines. One researcher found that the strokes used in vertical manuscript are the same as the shapes children use in their drawings (Farris, 1993). Because children are familiar with these shapes, they can identify and form the strokes with little difficulty.

Slanted manuscript can create problems with legibility

Legibility is an important goal in handwriting. Obviously, content should not be sacrificed for legibility, but what is handwriting if it cannot be read?

Educational researchers have tested the legibility of slanted manuscript and found that children writing vertical manuscript "performed significantly better" than those writing slanted manuscript. The writers of the slanted alphabet tended to make more misshapen letterforms, tended to extend their strokes above and below the guidelines, and had a difficult time keeping their letterforms consistent in size (Graham, 1992).

On the other hand, the vertical manuscript style of print has a lot of support in the area of research. Advertisers have known for years that italic type has a lower readability rate than vertical "roman" type. Research shows that in 30 minute readings, the italic style is read 4.9% slower than roman type (14–16 words per minute). This is why most literature, especially literature for early readers, is published using roman type.

Slanted manuscript can impair letter recognition

Educators have suspected that it would be beneficial for students to write and read the same style of alphabet. In other words, if children *read* vertical manuscript, they should also *write* vertical manuscript. Now it has been found that inconsistent alphabets may actually be detrimental to children's learning.

Researchers have found that slanted manuscript impairs the ability of some young children to recognize many letters. Some children who learn the slanted style alphabet find it difficult to recognize many of the traditional letterforms they see in books and environmental print. "[These children] consistently had difficulty identifying several letters, often making the same erroneous response to the same letter," the researchers reported. They concluded that slanted manuscript "creates substantially more letter recognition errors and causes more letter confusion than does the traditional style." (Kuhl & Dewitz, 1994).

Slanted manuscript does not help with transition

One of the benefits proposed by the creators of the slanted manuscript alphabet was that it made it easier for children to make the transition from manuscript to cursive writing. However, no difference in transition time has been found between the two styles of manuscript alphabets. In addition, the slanted style does not seem to enhance young children's production of cursive letters (Graham, 1992).

> " *...slanted manuscript letters cannot be recommended as a replacement for the traditional manuscript alphabet.* "

The slanted style of manuscript appeared to be a good idea. But educators should take a close look at what the research shows before adopting this style of alphabet. As one researcher has said, "Given the lack of supportive evidence and the practical problems involved in implementation, slanted manuscript letters cannot be recommended as a replacement for the traditional manuscript alphabet" (Graham, 1994).

Farris, P.J. (1993). Learning to write the ABC's: A comparison of D'Nealian and Zaner-Bloser handwriting styles. *Indiana Reading Quarterly, 25* (4), 26–33.

Graham, S. (1992). Issues in handwriting instruction. *Focus on Exceptional Children, 25* (2).

Graham, S. (1994, Winter). Are slanted manuscript alphabets superior to the traditional manuscript alphabet? *Childhood Education,* 91–95.

Kuhl, D. & Dewitz, P. (1994, April). The effect of handwriting style on alphabet recognition. Paper presented at the annual meeting of the American Educational Research Association, New Orleans, LA.

Zaner-Bloser
Handwriting
With a new alphabet

Author

Clinton S. Hackney

Contributing Authors

Pamela J. Farris
Janice T. Jones
Linda Leonard Lamme

Zaner-Bloser, Inc.

P.O. Box 16764
Columbus, Ohio 43216-6764

Author
Clinton S. Hackney, Ed.D.

Contributing Authors
Pamela J. Farris, Ph.D.
Janice T. Jones, M.A.
Linda Leonard Lamme, Ph.D.

Reviewers
Judy L. Bausch, Grade 6, Columbus, Georgia
Cherlynn Bruce, Grade 1, Conroe, Texas
Karen H. Burke, Director of Curriculum and Instruction, Bar Mills, Maine
Anne Chamberlin, Grade 2, Lynchburg, Virginia
Carol J. Fuhler, Grade 6, Flagstaff, Arizona
Deborah D. Gallagher, Grade 5, Gainesville, Florida
Kathleen Harrington, Grade 3, Redford, Michigan
Rebecca James, Grade 3, East Greenbush, New York
Gerald R. Maeckelbergh, Principal, Blaine, Minnesota
Bessie B. Peabody, Principal, East St. Louis, Illinois

Marilyn S. Petruska, Grade 5, Coraopolis, Pennsylvania
Sharon Ralph, Kindergarten, Nashville, Tennessee
Linda E. Ritchie, Grade 4, Birmingham, Alabama
Roberta Hogan Royer, Grade 2, North Canton, Ohio
Marion Redmond Starks, Grade 2, Baltimore, Maryland
Elizabeth J. Taglieri, Grade 2, Lake Zurich, Illinois
Claudia Williams, Grade 6, Lewisburg, West Virginia

Credits
Art: Lizi Boyd: 6, 22–23, 28–29, 36–37, 40, 58–59, 70–71, 92–93, 106–107, 120–121; Denise & Fernando: 3–4, 6, 20–21, 34–35, 40, 47, 60–61, 78–79, 96–97, 110–111, 122; Gloria Elliott: 5, 16, 42; Michael Grejniec: 3, 7, 11, 24–25, 30–31, 41, 54–55, 68–69, 82–83, 100–101, 114–115; Shari Halpern: 1, 4, 6, 26–27, 32–33, 38–39, 40, 42–43, 62–63, 74–75, 84, 89, 102–103, 116–117, 126; Daniel Moreton: 86; Andy San Diego: 3, 6, 40, 56–57, 64–65, 72–73, 90–91, 104–105, 118–119, 124–125; Troy Viss: 4–5, 7, 16, 41, 66–67, 76–77, 80–81, 94–95, 98–99, 108–109, 112–113

Photos: John Lei/OPC: 8–9, 44–45; Stephen Ogilvy: 3–5, 10, 12–19, 23, 26–27, 32–33, 46, 48, 50–52, 56–57, 59, 62–63, 68–69, 74–75, 78–79, 82–83, 87–91, 96–97, 102–105, 107, 110–111, 114–115, 120, 123–125

Developed by Kirchoff/Wohlberg, Inc., in cooperation with Zaner-Bloser Publishers
Cover illustration by Shari Halpern

ISBN 0-88085-706-4

Copyright © 1996 Zaner-Bloser, Inc.

Teacher Edition Artists
Lizi Boyd; Denise & Fernando; Shari Halpern; Diane Paterson; Andy San Diego

CONTENTS

Manuscript
Unit I Getting Started

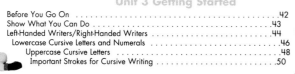

Unit 2 Writing in Manuscript

Cursive
Unit 3 Getting Started

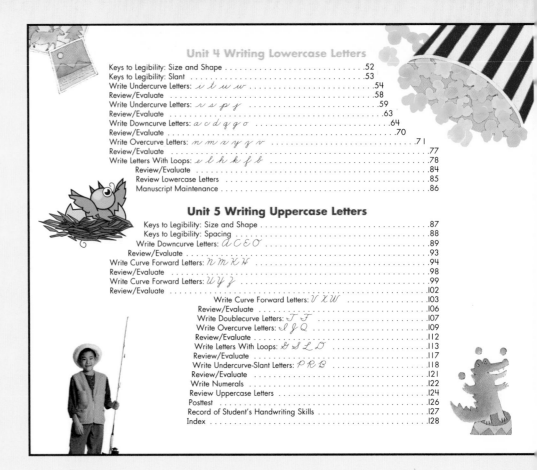

Follow the path. Write each letter you find.

start ➡ i w t r e finish

What can the letters spell?
Write the word and read the message.

Let's _____.

In this book, you will find letters, words, and
sentences to write. You will learn how to make
your manuscript writing easy for you and for
others to read.

Before You Go On

5

HOW THIS BOOK IS ORGANIZED

The **Getting Started** pages will help students learn the vocabulary and conventions of this handwriting program.

In **Writing in Manuscript**, lower-case and uppercase letters are presented together. The letter sequence is determined by common elements of the lowercase letters. Note that models are provided and students have space to write directly beneath the models. My Own Words provides an opportunity for students to write familiar words and On Your Own encourages them to write about their own experiences.

In **Writing in Cursive**, lowercase letters are presented before uppercase letters. As in manuscript, letter sequence is determined by common elements. Models are provided and students write directly beneath the models.

Point out that students will evaluate their handwriting frequently. Set up a portfolio for each student to assess individual progress throughout the year.

Preview the book with your students. Use this page with your class as an introduction to the Zaner-Bloser handwriting program. Call attention to writing from the maze and help them figure out the message.

PRACTICE MASTERS FOR UNIT 1

- Letter to Parents—English, 78
- Letter to Parents—Spanish, 79
- Manuscript Alphabet—English, 86
- Manuscript Alphabet—Spanish, 88
- Record of Student's Handwriting Skills, 74
- Zaner-Bloser Handwriting Grid, 126

Share the verse on the page with your students. Discuss with students the different kinds of writing they do. Ask them to write the lines of this poem in their best handwriting on the next page.

Pretest

I Can

I can write a story.
I can write a poem.
I can write at school,
And I can write at home.

6

After they write, explain to students that at a future date, they will be asked to write this poem again and compare it with the writing they do today.

Ask students to keep their pretests in their books or writing portfolios for comparison with their posttests later in the year.

EVALUATE

Observe as students write, and informally assess their present handwriting skills. Then guide them to talk about their writing and to explain why they chose one line of writing as their best.

I Can

I can write a story.
I can write a poem.
I can write at school,
And I can write at home.

Write the poem in your best handwriting.

Put a star next
to your best line
of writing.

7

COACHING HINT

Make a desktop nametag for each student in your class, using tagboard or self-adhesive ruled strips. Tape the nametags to the students' desks so they can use them as writing models. (visual)

ABCs of Writing Ideas

Discuss with students the various kinds of writing they might do at different times. Brainstorm a list of things they might write. If your students like a challenge, ask them to think of one idea for each letter of the alphabet. Here are some ideas to get started:

alphabet books
brochures
cartoons
diaries
envelopes
friendly letters
greeting cards

Display the list so students can refer to it often. (visual, auditory)

Take a Good Look

Take a walk with your class through the classroom or school building. Ask students to look for examples of environmental print. After touring, make a chart of your findings. List the messages and the places where they appeared. Add to this list as students become aware of other print in their environment. (visual)

Invite students to play a game of "Simon Says." Give students directions that include the words *left* and *right*. Have them stand facing you. Remind them to follow the direction only when they hear "Simon says." Begin with these:

Simon says, "Touch your head with your right hand."
Touch your nose with your left hand.
Simon says, "Take two giant steps to the left."

Note if any students have difficulty distinguishing left from right.

Left

If you write with your left hand . . .

Sit up tall.

Hold your pencil like this.

Slant your paper.

8

Work through these pages with the students.

Demonstrate how to place both arms on the desk, with only the elbows off the desk, and how to sit up straight.

Demonstrate the correct way to hold a pencil for both left-handers and right-handers.

Distribute paper with guidelines and help students follow the directions for proper paper position.

Let students use what they have learned by writing their names or a sentence on the paper.

If you write with your right hand . . .

Sit up tall.

Hold your pencil like this.

Keep your paper straight.

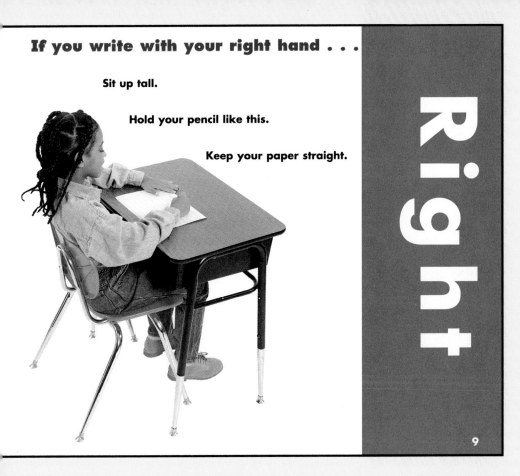

Right

9

COACHING HINT

Right-handed teachers will better understand left-handed students if they practice the left-handed position themselves. The Zaner-Bloser Writing Frame can be used to show good hand position because the hand automatically settles into the correct position. Group left-handed writers together for instruction if you can do so without calling attention to the practice. They should be seated to the left of the chalkboard.

Left Hand, Right Hand, or Both?

Ask students to listen to the following directions and to pantomime the activities, using the hand you name.

Pick up a pencil with your left hand.
Comb your hair with your right hand.
Catch a ball with both hands.
Write with your right hand.
Draw with your left hand.
Lift a box with both hands.

(auditory, kinesthetic)

Set the Table

Explain to students that knowing about left and right is important for more than just writing. Distribute large sheets of manila paper and crayons. Tell students that the paper represents a place mat and they will help set the table by drawing what is needed. Demonstrate at the chalkboard. Ask students to draw a plate in the center of the mat. Then ask them to draw a fork to the left of the plate and a knife and a spoon to the right of the plate. (visual, kinesthetic)

Check students' letter knowledge with an identification game. Ask them to point to letters on the page as you ask questions such as these:

Which lowercase letters are tall?
Which uppercase letters have slant lines?
Which uppercase letters look very different from their lowercase partner?
Which uppercase letters look similar to their lowercase partner?

Continue with questions about numerals.

Practice Masters 86 and 88 are available for use with these pages.

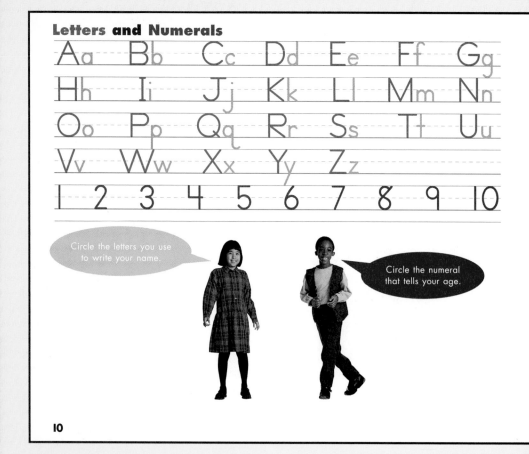

Letters and Numerals

Aa Bb Cc Dd Ee Ff Gg
Hh Ii Jj Kk Ll Mm Nn
Oo Pp Qq Rr Ss Tt Uu
Vv Ww Xx Yy Zz
1 2 3 4 5 6 7 8 9 10

Circle the letters you use to write your name.

Circle the numeral that tells your age.

10

Work through these pages with the students.

Guide students in locating and naming each guideline. Have them name its color and tell whether the line is solid or broken. Explain that using guidelines will help them write better letters.

Have students take turns naming the letters they use to write their names.

Review that tall letters touch both the headline and the baseline. Call attention to the fact that all the uppercase letters are tall. Ask students for other examples of tall letters.

To review short letters, explain that short letters touch the midline and the baseline. Ask students for examples of short letters.

Point out that some short letters like **g** go below the baseline and touch the headline of the next writing line. Ask students for examples of other short letters that go below the baseline.

Tall letters touch the headline.
All uppercase letters are tall.
Circle the tall letters.

b c d D v F h m

Letters are tall or short.

Short letters touch the midline.
Circle the short letters.

a c f i P n o

Some letters go below the baseline.
Circle the letters that go below the baseline.

g j J G p q y x X

Write your name. Remember to begin with an uppercase letter.

_____

Write the age you will be on your next birthday.

EVALUATE

Invite students to compare the letters and numerals they wrote with the models they circled on the page.

To help students evaluate their writing, ask questions such as these:
Did you begin your name with an uppercase letter?
Does your uppercase letter begin at, or just below, the headline?
Does your uppercase letter rest on the baseline?
Did you use lowercase letters to write your name?
Does your numeral touch the headline and baseline?

Invite students to tell which letters they used and how the guidelines helped them.

COACHING HINT

Refer students to these pages often as a guide for writing. Students will find them especially helpful when they write independently.

The development of self-evaluation skills is an important goal of handwriting instruction. It helps students become independent learners. By having students compare their letters with models, you have already begun this process. Be patient. Some students will be more able than others to evaluate their writing.

FUN and GAMES

Letter Town, USA
Invite students to make a set of tactile alphabet letter cards for a bulletin board display. Print each letter pair (uppercase and lowercase) on a blank index card and distribute the cards. Ask students to cover the letters with glue and then add glitter or small pieces of macaroni. Label the bulletin board *Letter Town, USA,* and invite students to visit and touch the letters often. (visual, kinesthetic)

Tall or Short?
Prepare a set of uppercase and lowercase alphabet letter cards and place them in a box. Include a set of numerals from 1 to 10. Write the headings *Tall* and *Short* on the chalkboard. Invite students to take turns selecting a card from the box and attaching it to the board under the correct heading. (visual)

Tell students they will be looking for two kinds of straight lines on these pages.

One line stands up straight and is made with a pull down straight stroke. The other line lies down straight and is made with a slide right or slide left stroke.

MODEL

Write pull down straight strokes on guidelines on the chalkboard. Model writing pull down straight strokes in the air and have students write in the air with you.

Follow the same procedure for slide right and slide left strokes.

12

Pull Down Straight Lines
Trace each pull down straight line.

L h I l i T n 5 g

Write these letters and numerals.

a B d t E 9 r H 4 F

Write these sentences.

I like to write.

This is my best writing.

Circle the letters with pull down straight lines.

12

Pull Down Straight Lines
Work through this page with the students.

First, ask students to look for the pull down straight lines in the letters and numerals. Have them trace each pull down straight line from top to bottom with a finger or the nonwriting end of a pencil.

Then help them complete the page.

Slide Right and Slide Left Lines

Trace each slide right and slide left line.

L F H I G 7 t e 2

Write these letters and numerals.

e f t E 2 J H T G Z 5

Write these sentences.

September is a fall month.

Winter starts in December.

Circle the letters with slide right lines.

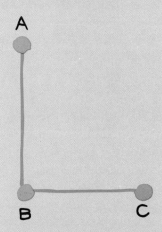

13

Slide Right and Slide Left Lines

As you work through this page with the students, first ask them to look for slide right and slide left lines in the letters and numerals. Have them trace each slide right or slide left line with a finger or the non-writing end of a pencil.

Then help them complete the page.

COACHING HINT

Have students name objects in the room formed with vertical lines. Explain that vertical lines are straight up and down. If possible, have students trace the lines with pull down straight strokes. (visual, kinesthetic)

ABC Connect the Dots

Make a dot-to-dot series on the chalkboard and label each dot with an uppercase alphabet letter. Provide colored chalk for students to use. Choose volunteers to connect two labeled dots with either a pull down straight stroke or a slide right or slide left stroke as you give directions. (auditory, kinesthetic)

A

B   C

Construct a Letter

Ask students to name the letters that are formed with only pull down straight and slide right or slide left strokes. List them (E, F, H, I, l, L, t, T) on the chalkboard. Cut construction paper into strips about one-half inch by three inches. Distribute strips and some glue. Demonstrate how to form a letter by gluing strips together. Tell students they will need to trim some strips. Have them make as many of the letters as time allows. (visual, kinesthetic)

BEFORE WRITING

Tell students they will be looking for circle lines and slant lines on these pages.

Draw two circles on the chalkboard. Show where a backward circle line begins by marking a starting place, at about one o'clock, with a star. Ask students to begin at the star and use their index fingers to trace over the line.

Show where a forward circle line begins by marking a starting place, at about nine o'clock, with a star. Ask students to begin at the star and use their index fingers to trace over the line.

Ask students to watch as you draw a series of slant right lines on the chalkboard. Ask in which direction the lines slant. Repeat for slant left lines.

MODEL

Use your arms to model making backward circles (left) and forward circles (right) and have students copy you.

Write slant right and slant left strokes on guidelines on the chalkboard. Model writing the strokes in the air and have students write in the air with you.

14

Circle Lines
Trace each circle line.

C 8 e a O b g d p

Write these letters and numerals.

o S s p 6 3 c D h Q

Write these sentences.

Pizza tastes good.

Peanut butter is better.

Circle the letters with circle lines.

14

Circle Lines
Work through this page with the students.

First, ask students to look for the circle lines in the letters and numerals. Have them trace each circle line with a finger or the nonwriting end of a pencil.

Then help them complete the page.

Slant Lines

Trace each slant line.

W Q A y X v w k 7

Write these letters and numerals.

w Y V K Z x M N y 7 2

Write these sentences.

My favorite color is green.

Blue and yellow make green.

Circle the letters with slant lines.

15

Slant Lines

Work through this page with the students.

First, ask students to look for the slant lines in the letters and numerals. Have students trace each slant line with a finger or the nonwriting end of a pencil.

Then help them complete the page.

COACHING HINT

Use an overhead projector to show pull down straight, slide right and slide left, circle, and slant lines. Ask students to wet their fingers in a cup of water and trace the enlarged lines on the chalkboard. (kinesthetic)

FUN and GameS

Lines and Designs

Distribute drawing paper and crayons. Play some lively music and ask students to draw as they listen. Then stop the music. Have students share their drawings. As students show their work, ask classmates to identify lines that were formed with any of the basic strokes: pull down straight, slide right, slide left, circle backward, circle forward, slant left, slant right. (visual)

Make and Shape Letters

Assign each student a letter pair (uppercase and lowercase) and distribute modeling clay. Have students form the letter pair with clay. When the letters are completed, assemble them on a table for a guessing game. Ask volunteers to close their eyes, trace a letter pair with a finger, and name the letter. (kinesthetic)

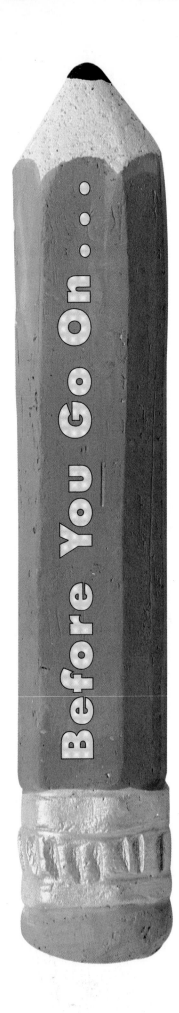

Before You Go On . . . .

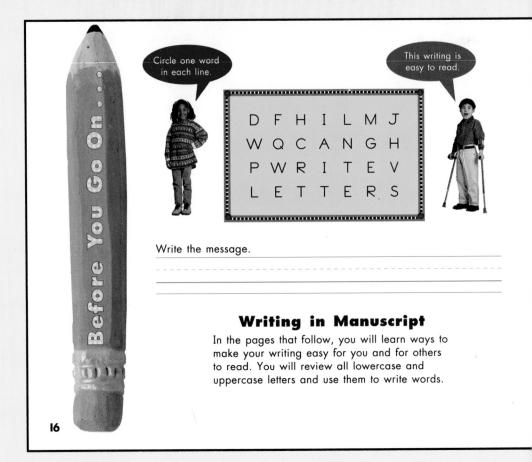

Circle one word in each line.

This writing is easy to read.

D F H I L M J
W Q C A N G H
P W R I T E V
L E T T E R S

Write the message.

Writing in Manuscript

In the pages that follow, you will learn ways to make your writing easy for you and for others to read. You will review all lowercase and uppercase letters and use them to write words.

16

Use this page to introduce your students to the **Writing in Manuscript** section of the book. After students write the message from the word puzzle, discuss the content of this section.

PREVIEW

Preview this section by calling attention to these features:
- letter models with numbered directional arrows
- guidelines for writing directly beneath handwriting models
- **My Own Words** writing space for familiar words
- opportunities for evaluating writing
- **On Your Own** activities with directions for independent writing

PRACTICE MASTERS FOR UNIT 2
- Manuscript Letters, 1–18
- Manuscript Numerals, 19–20
- Certificates, 75–77
- Manuscript Alphabet—English, 86
- Manuscript Alphabet—Spanish, 88
- Manuscript Stroke Descriptions—English, 90–93
- Manuscript Stroke Descriptions—Spanish, 94–97
- Record of Student's Handwriting Skills, 74
- Zaner-Bloser Handwriting Grid, 126

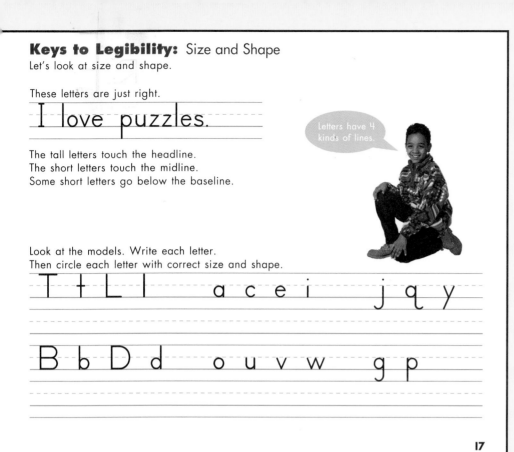

Keys to Legibility: Size and Shape

Let's look at size and shape.

These letters are just right.

I love puzzles.

Letters have 4 kinds of lines.

The tall letters touch the headline.
The short letters touch the midline.
Some short letters go below the baseline.

Look at the models. Write each letter.
Then circle each letter with correct size and shape.

T t L l   a c e i   j q y

B b D d   o u v w   g p

17

The keys to legibility are introduced on pages 17, 18, and 19. You may wish to work through these pages with your students.

MODEL THE WRITING

Write guidelines on the chalkboard. Have volunteers identify and name each guideline. Write an example of a tall letter, a short letter, and a letter that goes below the baseline. Ask students to name each letter and describe its size. Explain that writing letters the correct size and shape are two keys to making writing easy to read.

EVALUATE

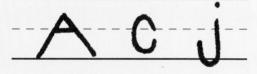

A C J

To help students evaluate the size and shape of their writing, ask questions such as these:
Do your tall letters touch the headline?
Do your short letters touch the midline?
Do letters that go below the baseline touch the next headline?
Are your letters easy to read?

COACHING HINT

Prepare a set of cards with lowercase alphabet letters. Have a student or group of students sort the letters by size. Remind students that **g, j, p, q,** and **y** are short letters that go below the baseline. (visual)

Keys to Legibility: Slant

Let's look at slant.

These letters are just right.

I love to pretend.

The letters are straight up and down.

Look at letters with pull down straight strokes.

Look at the models. Write each word.
Then circle each word in which the letters are straight up and down.

sing   act   dance   shout

jump   twirl   skip   clap

MODEL THE WRITING

Ask students to stand up as straight as they can and imagine a straight line drawn from their heads to their feet. Explain that manuscript writing is straight up and down. Introduce the term *slant* to refer to this vertical quality. On guidelines on the chalkboard, write two words—one with letters that are straight up and down and one with letters that slant either left or right. Ask which example looks correct and have students explain why. Point out that writing letters straight up and down, with correct slant, is another key to making writing easy to read.

EVALUATE

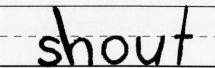

To help students evaluate the slant of their letters, ask questions such as these:
Look at the word *shout*. Are the pull down straight strokes in **h, u,** and **t** straight up and down?
Look at the word *twirl*. Are the pull down straight strokes in **t, i, r,** and **l** straight up and down?

COACHING HINT

You can evaluate the vertical quality of students' handwriting by drawing lines through the vertical strokes of the letters. If the lines are parallel, the vertical quality is correct.

Keys to Legibility: Spacing

Let's look at spacing.

These words are just right.

I love jokes.

> Look at spaces between letters and between words.

The letters are not too close.
The letters are not too far apart.
There is a finger space between words.

Look at the models. Write each word.
Then circle each word with correct letter spacing.

silly   funny   cute   long

Put a star next to the sentence with good word spacing.
Then write the sentence correctly.

I know a joke.   I know a   joke.

MODEL THE WRITING

On guidelines on the chalkboard, write *silly*, first with letters that are too close and then with letters that are too far apart. Ask students to explain what is wrong with the writing. Choose a volunteer to write the word with correct spacing. Add the word *jokes*, placing a finger between the words. Explain that writing with correct spacing between letters in a word, and between words, is another key to making writing easy to read.

EVALUATE

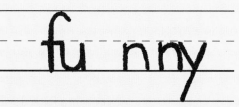

funny

To help students evaluate the spacing in their writing, ask questions such as these: Look at the word *funny*. Are the letters in the word too close or too far apart? Is there room for a finger space between the words *a* and *joke* in your sentence? Is your sentence easy to read?

COACHING HINT

Review the keys to legibility—size and shape, slant, and spacing. Provide colored chalk for students to use at the chalkboard. Have them take turns correcting and rewriting words with incorrect size and shape, slant, or spacing. (visual, kinesthetic)

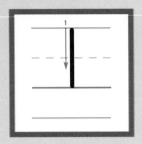

Touch the headline; pull down straight to the baseline.

Touch the midline; pull down straight to the baseline. Lift. Dot.

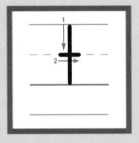

Touch the headline; pull down straight to the baseline. Lift. Touch the midline; slide right.

FuN and Games

Guess Who?

Have the students write their names on the chalkboard. Ask them to look for names that have l, i, or t. Play a guessing game with the names, for example: *I am thinking of a girl. Her name begins with L. There are two t's in her name. Who is she?* (auditory, visual, kinesthetic)

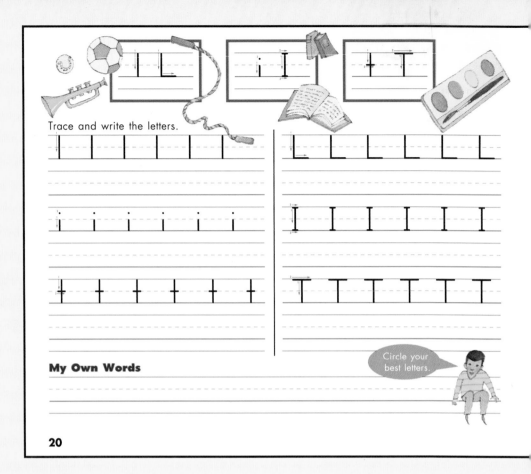

Trace and write the letters.

My Own Words

Circle your best letters.

MODEL THE WRITING

Write l, i, and t on guidelines as you say the stroke descriptions for each letter. Model writing the letters in the air as you repeat the descriptions. Have students say them as they write the letters in the air with you. Follow the same procedure for L, I, and T.

A CLOSER LOOK

Call attention to the size and shape of the letters by asking questions such as these:
Which letters are tall?
Which letter is short?
Which stroke begins each letter?
Which letters have a slide right stroke?

PRACTICE

Let students practice writing the letter pairs lL, iI, and tT on laminated writing cards or slates before they write on the pages.

Note: In each Evaluate section, the letter-forms illustrate common problems in letter formation.

EVALUATE

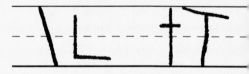

To help students evaluate their writing, ask questions such as these:
Is your l straight up and down?
Does your L begin at the headline?
Does your i begin at the midline?
Is your I about the same width as the model?
Is the slide right stroke of your t on the midline?
Are the strokes in your T straight?

BETTER LETTERS

To help students write pull down straight strokes correctly, remind them to pull, not draw, the strokes.

Write names of people.

Begin each name with an uppercase letter.

Lela

Ira

Tim

Ilse

Luis

Tatiana

On Your Own Write your full name.

Circle the name you wrote best.

21

WRITE LEGIBLY

Before students write, call attention to the size and shape of letters. Point out that names begin with uppercase letters and all uppercase letters are tall.

After they write, have them compare their letters with the models. Guide students to recognize why one name they wrote might be better than another.

COACHING HINT

To accommodate the needs of students with various modality strengths, introduce letters in three steps:
1. Talk about the letter—its size, shape, and strokes. (auditory)
2. Demonstrate the letter on the chalk-board. (visual)
3. Have students trace the letter in the air or on some other surface. (kinesthetic)

PRACTICE MASTERS 1–2

Trace and write.
I I I i i i t t t
lit   till   lime   built   listen
tail   lift   light   little   terrible
Write words you know.
Name
Copyright © Zaner-Bloser, Inc.   PRACTICE MASTER 1

Trace and write.
L L L I I I T T T
Luis and Ira are reading
Tamar and Lisa are talking
Write about what you are doing
Name
Copyright © Zaner-Bloser, Inc.   PRACTICE MASTER 2

CONTINUOUS STROKE

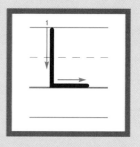

Touch the headline; pull down straight to the baseline. Slide right.

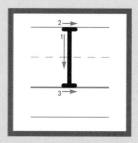

Touch the headline; pull down straight to the baseline. Lift. Touch the headline; slide right. Lift. Touch the baseline; slide right.

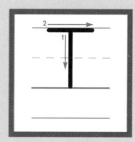

Touch the headline; pull down straight to the baseline. Lift. Touch the headline; slide right.

Write Away

Lucy Likes Lemonade
Invite students to say these alliterative sentences with you.

Lucy likes lemonade.
Ida is in Ireland.
Todd tied ten ties.

Ask students to write other alliterative sentences about Lucy, Ida, and Todd. (auditory)

Touch below the midline; circle back (left) all the way around.

Touch below the midline; circle back (left) all the way around. Push up straight to the midline. Pull down straight to the baseline.

Touch below the midline; circle back (left) all the way around. Push up straight to the headline. Pull down straight to the baseline.

Fun and Games

O, My Name Is . . .
Write this pattern on the chalkboard:

O, my name is (Olive).
I live in (Oklahoma),
and I like (ostriches).

Repeat the pattern with students, using aA and dD. (auditory, visual)

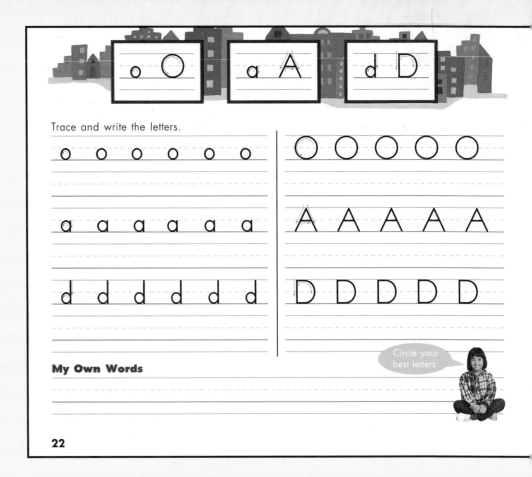

Trace and write the letters.

o o o o o o   O O O O O

a a a a a a   A A A A A

d d d d d d   D D D D D

My Own Words

Circle your best letters.

22

Model the Writing
Write o, a, and d on guidelines as you say the stroke descriptions for each letter. Have students use their fingers to trace the models o, a, and d in their books as you repeat the descriptions. Follow the same procedure for O, A, and D.

A Closer Look
Call attention to the size and shape of the letters by asking questions such as these:
Which letters are tall?
Which letters are short?
Which letters look alike except for their size?
Which letters begin with a backward circle stroke?
Which letters have slide right strokes?
Which letter has two slant strokes?

Practice
Let students practice writing the letter pairs oO, aA, and dD on laminated writing cards or slates before they write on the pages.

Evaluate

To help students evaluate their writing, ask questions such as these:
Are your o and O round?
Does your pull down straight stroke in a touch the circle?
Is your A about the same width as the model?
Is the backward circle in your d round?
Is your D about the same width as the model?

Better Letters

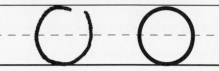

To help students make backward circle strokes correctly, remind them to close the circle properly.

Write names of cities.

Begin each name with an uppercase letter.

Oakland   Akron   Dallas

Atlanta   Orlando   Detroit

On Your Own
Write the name of the town or city and the state where you live.

Circle the name you wrote best.

WRITE LEGIBLY

Before students write, call attention to the spacing between letters in one of the names on the page. Help students conclude that none of the letters in the word touch.

After they write, have students compare their spacing of letters in words with the models. Guide students to recognize why one name they wrote might be better than another.

COACHING HINT

To help students understand the term *below*, make widely spaced guidelines on the floor with masking tape. Identify each guideline and label it. Then give directions for students to stand below the guideline you name. Invite students to "walk" the letters **o, O, a,** and **d** as you say the stroke descriptions. (auditory, kinesthetic)

PRACTICE MASTERS 3–4

Trace and write
o o o   a a a   d d d

odd road bedroom anybody

board door added about

Write words you know.

Name

Copyright © Zaner-Bloser, Inc.   PRACTICE MASTER 3

Trace and write
O O O   A A A   D D D

Omar likes to play soccer.

Ann and Di like to jump rope.

Write about outdoor games you like to play.

Name

Copyright © Zaner-Bloser, Inc.   PRACTICE MASTERS 4

CONTINUOUS STROKE

Touch below the headline; circle back (left) all the way around.

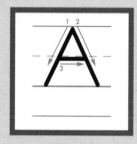

Touch the headline; slant left to the baseline. Lift. Touch the headline; slant right to the baseline. Lift. Touch the midline; slide right.

Touch the headline; pull down straight to the baseline. Lift. Touch the headline; slide right; curve forward (right) to the baseline; slide left.

Write Away

Away We Go!
Invite students to make a poster showing a favorite place in their town or city or a place they have visited. Then have them label the poster and add a caption, such as *Come Visit Us!* (visual)

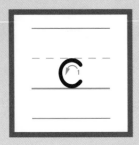

Touch below the midline; circle back (left), ending above the baseline.

Touch halfway between the midline and baseline; slide right; circle back (left), ending above the baseline.

Touch below the headline; curve back (left); pull down straight to the baseline. Lift. Touch the midline; slide right.

F u N and G ame S

Cats, Elephants, and Foxes

Invite students to draw a cat, an elephant, or a fox. Distribute writing paper and ask students to write words that begin with the same letter as the animal name. (visual, auditory, kinesthetic)

24

Trace and write the letters.

c c c c c c   C C C C C

e e e e e e   E E E E E E

f f f f f f   F F F F F F

My Own Words

Circle your best letters.

24

MODEL THE WRITING

Write **c**, **e**, and **f** on guidelines as you say the stroke descriptions. Invite students to use their index fingers to write these letters on their desks as you repeat the descriptions and they say them with you. Follow the same procedure for **C**, **E**, and **F**.

A CLOSER LOOK

Call attention to the size and shape of the letters by asking questions such as these:
Which letters are short?
Which letters are tall?
Which letters begin with a backward circle stroke?
Which letters begin with a pull down straight stroke?
Which letters look alike except for their size?

PRACTICE

Let students practice writing the letter pairs **cC**, **eE**, and **fF** on laminated writing cards or slates before they write on the pages.

EVALUATE

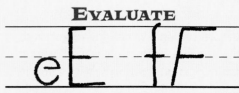

To help students evaluate their writing, ask questions such as these:
Do your **c** and **C** look like a circle that has not been closed?
Does your slide right stroke in **e** touch your circle back stroke?
Are the top and bottom slide right strokes in your **E** the same width?
Does your **f** begin below the headline?
Is your **F** straight up and down?

BETTER LETTERS

To help students write **c** and **C** correctly, place dots for the beginning and ending points of the letters.

Begin important words in each title with an uppercase letter.

Write titles of books. Underline the titles.

Clifford's Family

Caps for Sale

Ernest and Celestine's Picnic

On Your Own Write the title of a book you like.

Circle the title you wrote best.

Touch below the headline; circle back (left), ending above the baseline.

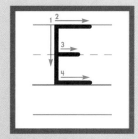

Touch the headline; pull down straight to the baseline. Lift. Touch the headline; slide right. Lift. Touch the midline; slide right. Stop short. Lift. Touch the baseline; slide right.

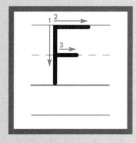

Touch the headline; pull down straight to the baseline. Lift. Touch the headline; slide right. Lift. Touch the midline; slide right. Stop short.

Write Away

Make Bookmarks
Invite students to make bookmarks about books they like. Have them write the book title and draw a picture to decorate an oak tag strip. (visual, kinesthetic)

WRITE LEGIBLY

Before students write, call attention to the spacing between words in the titles of the books. Remind students that the space shows where one word ends and another begins.

After they write, have students compare their spacing between words with the spacing in the models. Guide them to recognize why one title they wrote might be better than another.

COACHING HINT

Encourage students to write with vertical slant. If students write letters that are not vertical, check to see if they need practice with any of the following: positioning the paper correctly, pulling the downstrokes in the proper direction, shifting the paper as the writing line fills.

PRACTICE MASTERS 5–6

Trace and write
c c c   e e e   f f f

face   each   cakes   fence   feed

chief   feel   clean   factory   cheek

Write words you know.

Name
Copyright © Zaner-Bloser, Inc.   PRACTICE MASTER 5

Trace and write
C C C   E E E   F F F

Federico fried the fresh fish.

Cara and Ed cooked the corn.

Write about cooking jobs you can do.

Name
Copyright © Zaner-Bloser, Inc.   PRACTICE MASTER 6

Touch below the midline; circle back (left) all the way around. Push up straight to the midline. Pull down straight through the baseline; curve back (left).

Touch the midline; pull down straight through the baseline; curve back (left). Lift. Dot.

Touch below the midline; circle back (left) all the way around. Push up straight to the midline. Pull down straight through the baseline; curve forward (right).

F ᵘN and GameS

Charades

Write a noun that begins with **g, j,** or **q** on each of twelve index cards. Have each student choose a word and act it out until a classmate guesses it and writes it on the board. (visual)

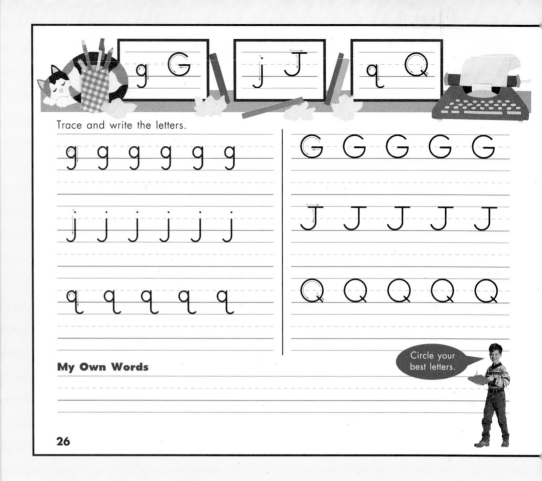

Trace and write the letters.

g g g g g g   G G G G G

j j j j j j   J J J J J

q q q q q q   Q Q Q Q Q

My Own Words

Circle your best letters.

26

MODEL THE WRITING

Write **g, j,** and **q** on guidelines as you say the stroke descriptions for each letter. Invite several students to dip a small sponge in water and use it to write these letters on the chalkboard while others say the descriptions with you. Follow the same procedure for **G, J,** and **Q.**

A CLOSER LOOK

Call attention to the size and shape of the letters by asking questions such as these:
Which letters are tall?
Which letters go below the baseline?
Which letters have a backward circle?
Which letters begin with a pull down straight stroke?
Which letter has a slide left stroke?

PRACTICE

Let students practice writing the letter pairs **gG, jJ,** and **qQ** on laminated writing cards or slates before they write on the pages.

EVALUATE

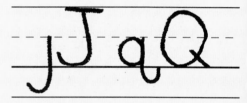

To help students evaluate their writing, ask questions such as these:
Is the backward circle of your **g** round?
Does the slide left stroke of your **G** touch the midline?
Did you remember to dot your **j**?
Is your **J** straight up and down?
Does your **q** touch the next headline?
Does your **Q** look like an **O** except for the slant right stroke?

BETTER LETTERS

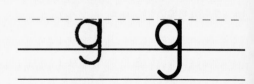

Remind students that descenders should fill the space below the baseline and touch the next headline.

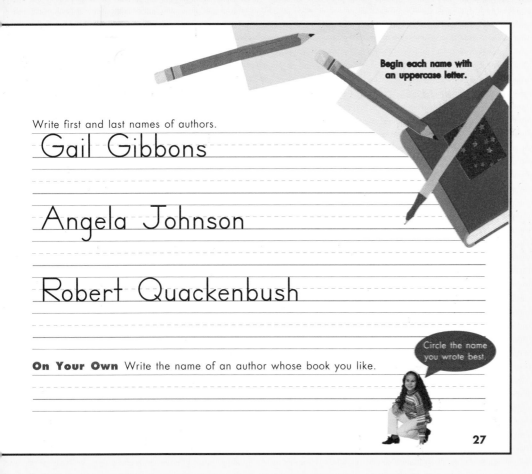

Write first and last names of authors.

Gail Gibbons

Angela Johnson

Robert Quackenbush

Begin each name with an uppercase letter.

On Your Own Write the name of an author whose book you like.

Circle the name you wrote best.

27

Touch below the headline; circle back (left), ending at the midline. Slide left.

Touch the headline; pull down straight; curve back (left). Lift. Touch the headline; slide right.

Touch below the headline; circle back (left) all the way around. Lift. Slant right to the baseline.

WRITE LEGIBLY

Before students write, call attention to the position of letters on the guidelines. Point out that **g, j,** and **q** are examples of short letters that go below the baseline and touch the next headline.

After they write, have students compare their letters with the models. Guide them to recognize why one name might be written better than another.

COACHING HINT

Write **g, j,** and **q** on guidelines on the chalkboard. Focus on the part of the letter that descends below the baseline. Have students trace over that part of each letter with colored chalk. Point out where the curve of each letter begins and ends. Explain that it rests on the headline of the next writing space. For further reinforcement, have students make **g, j,** and **q** from pipe cleaners or play dough. (visual, kinesthetic)

PRACTICE MASTERS 7–8

Trace and write
g g g   j j j   q q q
job quick great join garbage
quilt junk queen joy language
Write words you know
Name
Copyright © Zaner-Bloser, Inc.   PRACTICE MASTER 7

Trace and write
G G G   J J J   Q Q Q
Quentin tells Aunt Judy jokes.
Jonelle shops for Grandma
Write about what you could do for someone.
Name
Copyright © Zaner-Bloser, Inc.   PRACTICE MASTER 8

Write Away

Design a Book Jacket
Have students choose a familiar book and make a book jacket for it. Distribute drawing paper and markers. Ask that they include the title of the book, the author's name, and an illustration on the front cover. On the back, have them write about the book. (visual, kinesthetic)

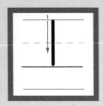

Touch the headline; pull down straight to the baseline.

Touch below the headline; curve forward (right); slant left to the baseline. Slide right.

Touch below the headline; curve forward (right) to the midline; curve forward (right), ending above the baseline.

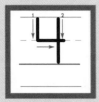

Touch the headline; pull down straight to the midline. Slide right. Lift. Move to the right and touch the headline; pull down straight to the baseline.

Touch the headline; pull down straight to the midline. Circle forward (right), ending above the baseline. Lift. Touch the headline; slide right.

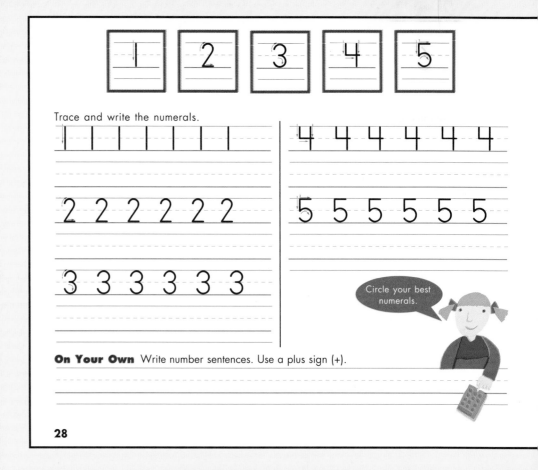

Trace and write the numerals.

On Your Own Write number sentences. Use a plus sign (+).

Circle your best numerals.

28

MODEL THE WRITING

Write 1, 2, 3, 4, and 5 on guidelines as you say the stroke descriptions for each numeral. Model writing the numerals in the air as you repeat the descriptions. Have students say them as they write the letters in the air with you. Follow the same procedure with 6, 7, 8, 9, and 10.

A CLOSER LOOK

Call attention to the size and shape of the numerals by asking questions such as these:
Do all these numerals touch the headline and baseline?
Which numerals have only straight lines?
Which numerals have slide right strokes?
Which numeral has two curve forward strokes?
Which numerals have a slant stroke?

PRACTICE

Let students practice writing the numerals 1, 2, 3, 4, 5, 6, 7, 8, 9, and 10 on laminated writing cards or slates before they write on the page.

EVALUATE

To help students evaluate their writing, ask questions such as these:
Is the pull down stroke in your 1 straight?
Is the slant left stroke in your 2 straight?
Are both parts of your 3 the same size?
Are the strokes in your 4 straight?
Does your 5 rest on the baseline?

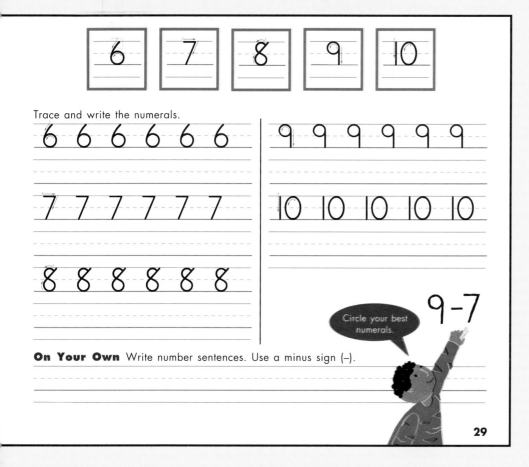

Trace and write the numerals.

6 6 6 6 6 6

9 9 9 9 9 9

7 7 7 7 7 7

10 10 10 10 10

8 8 8 8 8 8

Circle your best numerals.

9-7

On Your Own Write number sentences. Use a minus sign (–).

29

EVALUATE

To help students evaluate their writing, ask questions such as these:
Does your **6** begin at the headline with a curve down stroke?
Are both strokes of your **7** straight?
Are the curves of your **8** about the same size?
Does your **9** have a round backward circle?
Is there a space between **1** and **0** in your **10**?

COACHING HINT

Emphasize the importance of legible numeral formation whenever students write numerals. Discuss problems that can arise if numerals are not formed correctly. (visual, auditory)

PRACTICE MASTERS 19–20

Trace and write.
1 1 1   2 2 2   3 3 3
4 4 4   5 5 5
2 + 3 = 5   5 – 4 = 1

Write a number sentence. Use + or –

Name

Copyright © Zaner-Bloser, Inc.   PRACTICE MASTER 19

Trace and write.
6 6 6   7 7 7   8 8 8
9 9 9   10 10 10
6 + 4 = 10   9 – 7 = 2

Write a number sentence. Use + or –

Name

Copyright © Zaner-Bloser, Inc.   PRACTICE MASTER 20

Touch the headline; curve down to the baseline; curve up to the midline and around to close the circle.

Touch the headline; slide right. Slant left to the baseline.

Touch below the headline; curve back (left); curve forward (right), touching the baseline; slant up (right) to the headline.

Touch below the headline; circle back (left) all the way around. Pull down straight to the baseline.

Touch the headline; pull down straight to the baseline. Lift. Touch the headline; curve down to the baseline; curve up to the headline.

Touch the midline; pull down straight; curve forward (right); push up to the midline. Pull down straight to the baseline.

Touch below the midline; curve back (left); curve forward (right), ending above the baseline.

FuN and Games

Under the Umbrella
Draw a large umbrella and a winding snake on the chalkboard, or cut them from construction paper. Place the snake under the umbrella. Ask students to write words that begin with **u** or **s** on colorful squares of paper with guidelines and place them under the umbrella. (visual, kinesthetic)

30

Trace and write the letters.

u u u u u

U U U U U

s s s s s

S S S S S

Circle your best letters.

My Own Words

MODEL THE WRITING

Write **u** and **s** on guidelines as you say the stroke descriptions for each letter. Have students use their fingers to trace the models in their books as you repeat the descriptions. Follow the same procedure for **U** and **S**.

A Closer Look

Call attention to the size and shape of the letters by asking questions such as these:
Which letters are short?
Which letters have curve backward and curve forward strokes?
How are **s** and **S** different?
Which letter ends on the baseline?
Which letter ends at the headline?

PRACTICE

Let students practice writing the letter pairs **uU** and **sS** on laminated writing cards or slates before they write on the pages.

EVALUATE

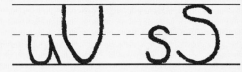

To help students evaluate their writing, ask questions such as these:
Are the pull down straight strokes in your **u** straight?
Does the curve of your **U** begin and end halfway between the midline and baseline?
Does your **s** begin just below the midline?
Is the top of your **S** about the same size as the bottom?

BETTER LETTERS

To help students make **s** (or **S**) correctly, make two circles, one on top of the other, then outline the curves.

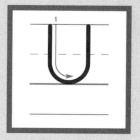

Begin important words in each title with an uppercase letter.

Write titles of songs. Use quotation marks— " and ".

"Six Little Ducks"

"When You Wish Upon a Star"

"Under the Sea"   "Sing"

On Your Own Write the title of a song you like to sing.

Circle the title you wrote best.

31

Touch the headline; pull down straight; curve forward (right); push up to the headline.

Touch below the headline; curve back (left); curve forward (right), ending above the baseline.

WRITE LEGIBLY

Before students write, call attention to the size and shape of tall letters. Point out that tall letters are written between the headline and baseline and that all uppercase letters are tall.

After they write, have them compare the size of their letters to the models. Guide students to see why one title they wrote might be written better than another.

COACHING HINT

Making sandpaper letters and having students trace them as you say the stroke descriptions will be helpful to students who have problems with small-muscle coordination and difficulty in writing letters. Guide students' fingers as they trace the letters **uU** and **sS** in one continuous motion. Forming letters in a tray of smooth wet sand is another good way to practice continuous strokes. (kinesthetic)

PRACTICE MASTERS 9–10

Trace and write
u u u   s s s

busy use summer rustle upset

gums rush sun music mouse

Write words you know.

Name

Copyright © Zaner-Bloser, Inc.   PRACTICE MASTER 9

Trace and write
U U U   S S S

Una uses an umbrella.

Simon wears a shiny slick coat.

Write about how you stay dry when it rains.

Name

Copyright © Zaner-Bloser, Inc.   PRACTICE MASTER 10

Write Away

Sing! Sing! Sing!
Brainstorm names of familiar children's songs. Then ask students to write two of their favorites on handwriting paper. Collect the papers, and write the lyrics to the songs on chart paper so students can follow along as they sing. Sing a few songs each day until all their favorites have been sung. (auditory, visual)

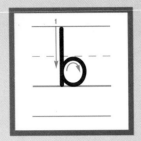

Touch the headline; pull down straight to the baseline. Push up; circle forward (right) all the way around.

Touch the midline; pull down straight through the baseline to the next guideline. Push up; circle forward (right) all the way around.

Touch the midline; pull down straight to the baseline. Push up; curve forward (right).

Fᵁ N and Games

Guess What?
Ask *What has long floppy ears and hops?* Choose a student to write the answer on the board. Point out that the answer begins with **r** (rabbit) or **b** (bunny). Then have students take turns asking one-sentence riddle questions. (auditory, kinesthetic)

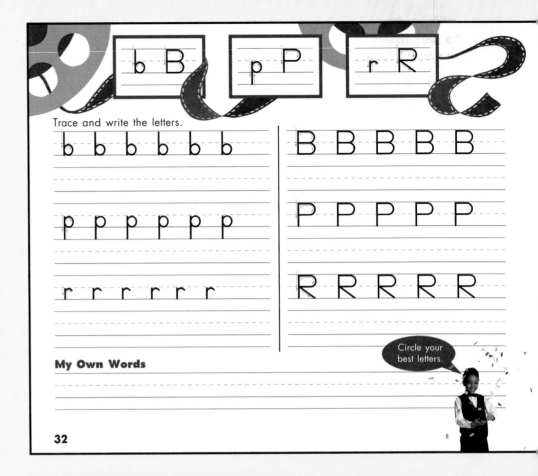

Trace and write the letters.

b b b b b b   B B B B B

p p p p p p   P P P P P

r r r r r r   R R R R R

My Own Words

Circle your best letters.

32

MODEL THE WRITING
Write **b**, **p**, and **r** on guidelines as you say the stroke descriptions for each letter. Invite students to use their index fingers to trace the letters on sandpaper as they repeat the descriptions with you. Follow the same procedure for **B**, **P**, and **R**.

A CLOSER LOOK
Call attention to the size and shape of the letters by asking questions such as these:
Which stroke is used to begin all the letters?
Which letter goes below the baseline?
Which letters have a push up stroke that retraces the pull down stroke?
Which letter has a slant stroke?
Which letters have slide left strokes?

PRACTICE
Let students practice writing the letter pairs **bB**, **pP**, and **rR** on laminated writing cards or slates before they write on the pages.

EVALUATE

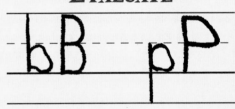

To help students evaluate their writing, ask questions such as these:
Does your **b** have a round forward circle?
Is your **B** about the same width as the model?
Is your forward circle in **p** round?
Are the slide right and slide left strokes in your **P** the same width?
Did you retrace carefully in your **r**?
Is your **R** straight up and down?

BETTER LETTERS

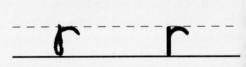

Remind students to push up (retrace) carefully to avoid making a loop when writing **r** and other letters with retraces.

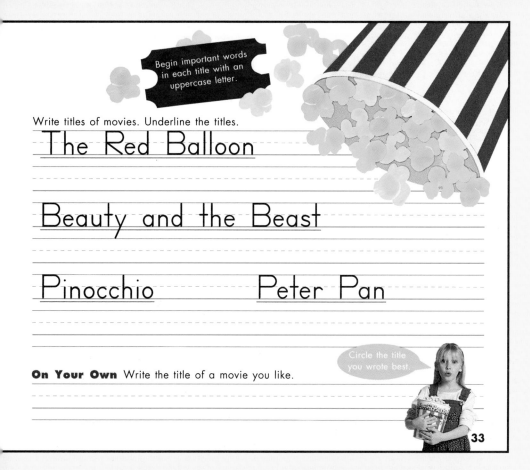

Write titles of movies. Underline the titles.

The Red Balloon

Beauty and the Beast

Pinocchio   Peter Pan

On Your Own Write the title of a movie you like.

Circle the title you wrote best.

33

Touch the headline; pull down straight to the baseline. Lift. Touch the headline; slide right; curve forward (right) to the midline; slide left. Slide right; curve forward (right) to the baseline; slide left.

Touch the headline; pull down straight to the baseline. Lift. Touch the headline; slide right; curve forward (right) to the midline; slide left.

Touch the headline; pull down straight to the baseline. Lift. Touch the headline; slide right; curve forward (right) to the midline; slide left. Slant right to the baseline.

WRITE LEGIBLY

Before students write, call attention to the slant of the letters. Remind students that manuscript letters are written straight up and down. Demonstrate by writing **b** once in correct vertical position and once slanting left. Ask a volunteer to circle the correct one.

After students write, have them compare their letters with the models to see if their letters are straight up and down. Guide students to recognize why one title they wrote might be written better than another.

COACHING HINT

To help avoid confusion about when to use a backward circle or a forward circle, explain that if a circle in a letter comes before the vertical stroke, it is always a backward circle, as in **a, d, g,** and **q.** If a vertical stroke in a letter comes before the circle, the circle is always a forward circle, as in **b** and **p.** (visual)

PRACTICE MASTERS 11–12

Trace and write
b b b   p p p   r r r

barn drip robber bulb problem

rope purple bump parade repair

Write words you know

Name

Copyright © Zaner-Bloser, Inc.   PRACTICE MASTER 11

Trace and write
B B B   P P P   R R R

Pablo practiced the piano.

Betty and Reva played drums.

Write about how you would like to make music.

Name

Copyright © Zaner-Bloser, Inc.   PRACTICE MASTER 12

Write Away

Invite children to make up a title for a new movie. Ask them to write a list of characters for the movie. (kinesthetic)

Touch the midline; pull down straight to the baseline. Push up; curve forward (right); pull down straight to the baseline.

Touch the midline; pull down straight to the baseline. Push up; curve forward (right); pull down straight to the baseline. Push up; curve forward (right); pull down straight to the baseline.

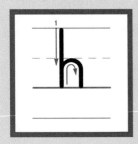

Touch the headline; pull down straight to the baseline. Push up; curve forward (right); pull down straight to the baseline.

FᵘN and GameS

Sense or Nonsense?
Write a story on the chalkboard with fill-in blanks. Ask students to write words or phrases that begin with **n**, **m**, or **h**. (visual)

34

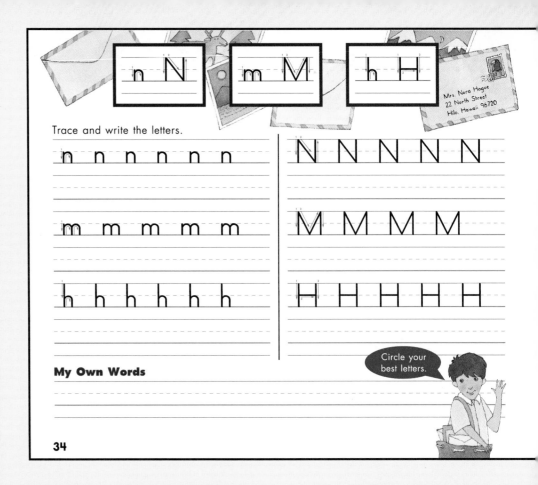

Trace and write the letters.

n n n n n n   N N N N N

m m m m m   M M M M

h h h h h h   H H H H H

My Own Words

Circle your best letters.

34

MODEL THE WRITING
Write **n**, **m**, and **h** on guidelines as you say the stroke descriptions for each letter. Invite several students to dip small sponges in water and to use them to write these letters on the chalkboard while others say the descriptions with you. Follow the same procedure for **N**, **M**, and **H**.

A CLOSER LOOK
Call attention to the size and shape of the letters by asking questions such as these:
Which stroke begins **N**, **M**, and **H**?
Which letters have slant right strokes?
Which letter has a slide right line?
Which lowercase letter is a tall letter?
Which letters have a curve forward stroke?

PRACTICE
Let students practice writing the letter pairs **nN**, **mM**, and **hH** on laminated writing cards or slates before they write on the pages.

EVALUATE

To help students evaluate their writing, ask questions such as these:
Are the pull down straight strokes in your **n** straight?
Is your **N** about the same width as the model?
Does the curve forward stroke of your **h** touch the midline?
Does the slide right stroke of your **H** touch the midline?

BETTER LETTERS

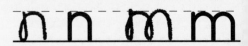

Remind students to push up (retrace) carefully to avoid making loops when writing **n** and **m**.

Write special titles and names of people.

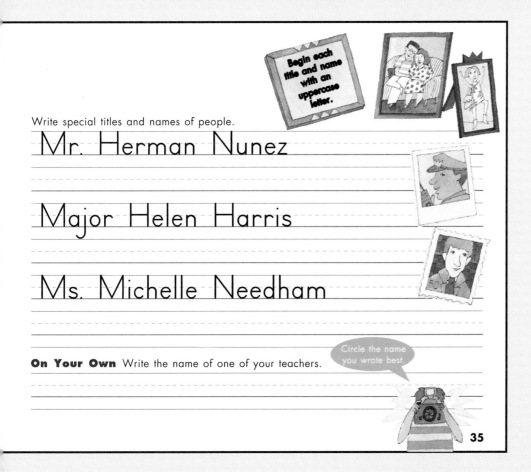

Mr. Herman Nunez

Major Helen Harris

Ms. Michelle Needham

On Your Own Write the name of one of your teachers.

Begin each title and name with an uppercase letter.

Circle the name you wrote best.

35

Touch the headline; pull down straight to the baseline. Lift. Touch the headline; slant right to the baseline. Push up straight to the headline.

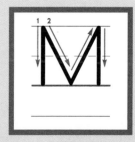

Touch the headline; pull down straight to the baseline. Lift. Touch the headline; slant right to the baseline. Slant up (right) to the headline. Pull down straight to the baseline.

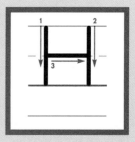

Touch the headline; pull down straight to the baseline. Lift. Move to the right and touch the headline; pull down straight to the baseline. Lift. Move to the left and touch the midline; slide right.

WRITE LEGIBLY

Before students write, call attention to the end marks that follow special titles used with people's names. Have the titles with end marks read aloud.

After students write, have them compare their writing with the models. Guide students to recognize why one name might be written better than another.

COACHING HINT

You can help evaluate the vertical quality of students' handwriting by drawing lines through the vertical strokes of their letters. If the lines are parallel, the vertical quality is correct. (visual)

PRACTICE MASTERS 13–14

Trace and write.
n n n   m m m   h h h

name horn thumb night machine

main shine hammer home nowhere

Write words you know.

Name

Copyright © Zaner-Bloser, Inc.   PRACTICE MASTER 13

Trace and write.
N N N   M M M   H H H

Hank made a map of Malta.

Nuncia has a model of Hawaii.

Write about a place you like.

Name

Copyright © Zaner-Bloser, Inc.   PRACTICE MASTER 14

Write Away

Just a Note

Have children write a note to an adult, using the person's title. (kinesthetic)

35

Touch the midline; slant right to the baseline. Slant up (right) to the midline.

Touch the midline; slant right to the baseline. Lift. Move to the right and touch the midline; slant left through the baseline.

Touch the midline; slant right to the baseline. Slant up (right) to the midline. Slant right to the baseline. Slant up (right) to the midline.

FᵘN and GameS

Letters in Color
Have students practice writing v, y, w, and other letters using paints and cotton swabs. Ask them to form letters as you say the stroke descriptions. Then have students say the stroke descriptions as classmates write the letters. (auditory, kinesthetic)

Trace and write the letters.

My Own Words

Circle your best letters.

36

MODEL THE WRITING
Write **v**, **y**, and **w** on guidelines as you say the stroke descriptions for each letter. Model writing the letters in the air as you repeat the descriptions. Have students say them as they write the letters in the air with you. Follow the same procedure for **V**, **Y**, and **W**.

A CLOSER LOOK
Call attention to the size and shape of the letters by asking questions such as these:
Which stroke is used in all these letters?
Which letters look the same except for their size?
Which letters are short?
Which letter goes below the baseline?
Where do you start writing all these upper-case letters?

PRACTICE
Let students practice writing the letter pairs **vV**, **yY**, and **wW** on laminated writing cards or slates before they write on the pages.

EVALUATE

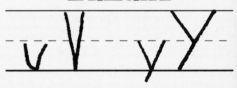

To help students evaluate their writing, ask questions such as these:
Are your slant strokes in **v** straight?
Is your **V** about the same width as the model?
Does your **y** touch the headline of the next space?
Does your **Y** end with a pull down straight stroke?
Are the slant strokes in your **w** straight?
Does your **W** begin at the headline?

BETTER LETTERS

Stress that all the strokes slant right.

Write names of holidays. Put an apostrophe (') in each one.

New Year's Eve

Valentine's Day

Washington's Birthday

Begin each word with an uppercase letter.

On Your Own Write about a holiday you like to celebrate.

Circle the holiday you wrote best.

37

WRITE LEGIBLY

Before students write, call attention to the spacing between words. Remind students to leave a finger space between words. After students write, have them compare their writing with the models. Guide students to recognize why the spacing in one holiday name might be better than the spacing in another.

COACHING HINT

If students have not mastered a handwriting skill or stroke, provide additional instruction and practice. Reinforce instruction with activities geared to each student's modality strengths. Help them evaluate their writing.

PRACTICE MASTERS 15–16

Trace and write

v v v   y y y   w w w

why   very   yawn   wrote   valley

way   yellow   weave   gravy   silver

Write words you know

Name

Copyright © Zaner-Bloser, Inc.   PRACTICE MASTER 15

Trace and write

V V V   Y Y Y   W W W

We all visited Vito's backyard

Yusuf wore his yellow vest

Write about what you like to wear

Name

Copyright © Zaner-Bloser, Inc.   PRACTICE MASTER 16

Touch the headline; slant right to the baseline. Slant up (right) to the headline.

Touch the headline; slant right to the midline. Lift. Move to the right and touch the headline; slant left to the midline. Pull down straight to the baseline.

Touch the headline; slant right to the baseline. Slant up (right) to the headline. Slant right to the baseline. Slant up (right) to the headline.

Write Away

Which Holiday Is It?
Invite students to name holidays they know. List them on the chalkboard. Have students choose one and write a description of an activity or an item they associate with the holiday. (visual, kinesthetic)

CONTINUOUS STROKE

Touch the midline; slant right to the baseline. Lift. Move to the right and touch the midline; slant left to the baseline.

Touch the headline; pull down straight to the baseline. Lift. Move to the right and touch the midline; slant left. Slant right to the baseline.

Touch the midline; slide right. Slant left to the baseline. Slide right.

FuN and Games

Listen and Write

On the chalkboard, write the spelling patterns *-ack, -ox,* and *-zz.* Give clues like those below and ask a student to write each answer under the correct pattern. *A boy's name ending in -ack. An animal ending in -ox. A sound a bee makes ending in -zz.* (visual, auditory, kinesthetic)

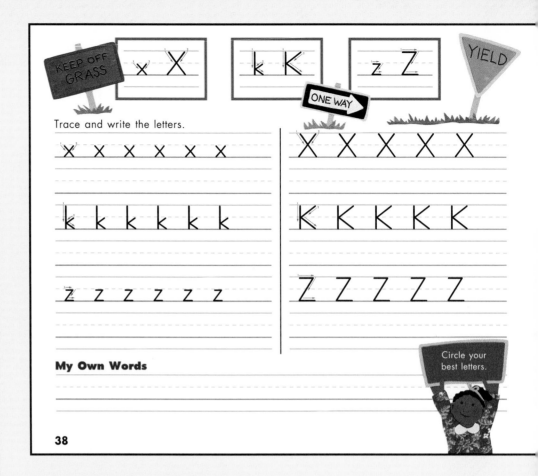

Trace and write the letters.

My Own Words

Circle your best letters.

MODEL THE WRITING

Write **x, k,** and **z** on guidelines as you say the stroke descriptions for each letter. Have students use their fingers to trace the models of these letters in their books as you repeat the descriptions. Follow the same procedure with **X, K,** and **Z.**

A CLOSER LOOK

Call attention to the size and shape of the letters by asking questions such as these:
Which letters are short?
Which letters are tall?
Which letters are alike except for size?
Which letters begin with a slide right stroke?
Which letters have a pull down straight stroke?

PRACTICE

Let students practice writing the letter pairs **xX, kK,** and **zZ** on laminated writing cards or slates before they write on the pages.

EVALUATE

To help students evaluate their writing, ask questions such as these:
Do your slant strokes in **x** cross halfway between the midline and baseline?
Do your slant strokes in **X** cross at the midline?
Do your two slant strokes in **k** meet halfway between the midline and baseline?
Do your two slant strokes in **K** meet at the midline?
Do your **z** and **Z** rest on the baseline?

BETTER LETTERS

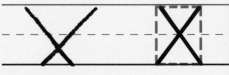

To ensure correct letter width, have students write the letter **x** or **X** and enclose it in a rectangle.

Write signs.

Shh! Children Snoozing!

Keep Off the Grass!   EXIT

Quiet Zone!   No Parking

On Your Own Write a sign for your classroom.

Circle the sign you wrote best.

39

Touch the headline; slant right to the baseline. Lift. Move to the right and touch the headline; slant left to the baseline.

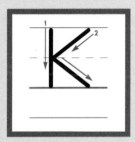

Touch the headline; pull down straight to the baseline. Lift. Move to the right and touch the headline; slant left to the midline. Slant right to the baseline.

Touch the headline; slide right. Slant left to the baseline. Slide right.

WRITE LEGIBLY

Before students write, call attention to the finger space between the words.

After students write, have them compare their word spacing with that of the models. Guide students to recognize why one sign they wrote might be better than another.

COACHING HINT

Review uppercase letters with slant strokes. Write **M, N, W, V, X,** and **K** on the chalkboard. Have students choose two letters to compare. Ask these questions: *How are they alike? How are they different? Which strokes are the same? Which letter has more strokes?* Repeat with circle letters **O, C, Q,** and **G** or straight line letters **L, I, T, E, F,** and **H**. (visual)

PRACTICE MASTERS 17–18

Trace and write.
x x x   k k k   z z z

like   wax   maze   zoom   kitchen

fix   knock   breeze   mixer   puzzle

Write words you know.

Name

Copyright © Zaner-Bloser, Inc.   PRACTICE MASTER 17

Trace and write.
X X X   K K K   Z Z Z

Kwaku kept nickels in a jar.

Xavier put Zoe's cake in a box.

Write about where you store things.

Name

Copyright © Zaner-Bloser, Inc.   PRACTICE MASTER 18

Write Away

Who's at the Zoo? Invite students to write a story about a yak, a zebra, and a kangaroo who live at the zoo and are friends. Suggest they draw a picture to accompany their story and include signs that might be found at the zoo. (visual, kinesthetic)

BEFORE WRITING

Invite students to share what they have accomplished in manuscript handwriting. Help them describe their progress in writing letters and words with correct size and shape, slant, and spacing.

Share the verse on the page with your students. Remind students that they wrote this verse at the beginning of the year. Explain that they will be writing the same lines today. Remind students to use correct letter size and shape, slant, and spacing as they write.

Manuscript Posttest

I Can
I can write a story.
I can write a poem.
I can write at school,
And I can write at home.

I Can
I can write a story.
I can write a poem.
I can write at school,
And I can write at home.

I Can
I can write a story.
I can write a poem.
I can write at school,
And I can write at home.

I Can

I can write a story.

I can write a poem.

I can write at school,

And I can write at home.

40

EVALUATE

Observe the students as they write. Help them compare this writing to the writing on the pretest, and discuss how their writing has changed or improved. Meet individually with students to help them assess their progress.

Certificates of Progress *should be awarded to those students who show notable handwriting progress and* Certificates of Excellence *to those who progress to the top levels of handwriting proficiency.*

I Can

I can write a story.
I can write a poem.
I can write at school,
And I can write at home.

Write the poem in your best handwriting.
Pay attention to size and shape, slant, and spacing.

Put a star next
to your best line
of writing.

41

Invite students to contribute ideas for topics they would like to write about. Include ideas for nonfiction and fiction. Organize the ideas on chart paper, and display the chart in your writing center. When students have free time, encourage them to choose a topic to write about and illustrate.

Ideas For Writing
Dinosaurs
Summer Vacation
Adventures
My Best Friend
The Circus

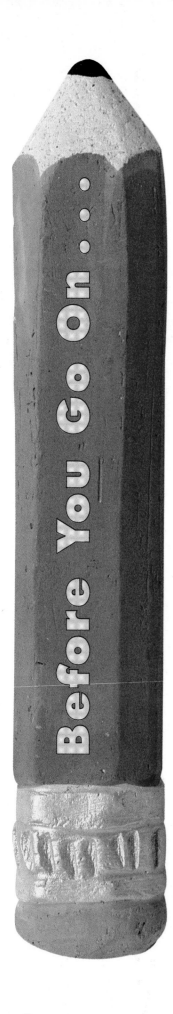

Get ready.   Get set.   *Go cursive.*

Writing in Cursive

At last! You're going to write in cursive.
As you learn cursive writing, you'll learn to
read it, too. The first thing you'll do is write
each letter. Then you'll join letters to write
words and sentences.

Try it. Write some letters you know in cursive.

42

Use this page to introduce your students to
the **Writing in Cursive** section of the book.
Students begin by showing what they can
write in cursive. The lessons that follow
review what students need to know to
develop good handwriting skills.

INTRODUCTION TO CURSIVE

The following are some criteria to help
determine whether a student is ready for
cursive writing.

Reading Level Does the student show
reading proficiency near grade level?

Manuscript Mastery Is the student able to
write legibly in manuscript?

Cursive Letter Recognition Is the student
able to recognize and identify all cursive
letters?

Cursive Word Reading Is the student able
to read cursive words?

Grouping of Letters Is the student able to
group letters according to size, shape,
beginning stroke, and ending stroke?

Understanding of Terminology Does the
student understand the terms for cursive
handwriting?

Understanding of Slant Does the student
understand that slant is determined by
paper position, the direction in which the
downstrokes are pulled, and the shifting of
the paper as the writing space is filled?

PRACTICE MASTERS FOR UNIT 3

- Letter to Parents—English, 80
- Letter to Parents—Spanish, 81
- Cursive Alphabet—English, 87
- Cursive Alphabet—Spanish, 89
- Record of Student's Handwriting Skills, 74
- Zaner-Bloser Handwriting Grid, 126

Show What You Can Do

Write your name in manuscript.

Now try writing your name in cursive.

What else can you write in cursive?
Write it here.

43

COACHING HINT: SELF-EVALUATION

Self-evaluation is an important step in the handwriting process. By identifying their own strengths and weaknesses, students become independent learners. Steps in the self-evaluation process are as follows:

1. Question
Students ask themselves questions such as these: "Is my slant correct?" "Do my letters rest on the baseline?"

2. Compare
Students compare their handwriting to correct models.

3. Evaluate
Students determine strengths and weaknesses in their handwriting based on the keys to legibility.

4. Diagnose
Students diagnose the cause of any difficulties. Possible causes include incorrect paper or pencil position, inconsistent pressure on pencil, and incorrect strokes.

5. Improve
Self-evaluation includes a means of improvement through additional instruction and continued practice. (visual, auditory, kinesthetic)

EVALUATE

As students write, monitor and informally assess their performance. Meet individually with students to help them assess their handwriting. Ask them how they would like to improve their writing.

LEFT-HANDED WRITERS RIGHT-HANDED WRITERS

Suggest that students refer to these pages throughout the year as a reminder of proper posture and correct paper and pencil position. Demonstrate correct positions for both left-handed and right-handed writers. Then ask students to place a sheet of paper in the proper position on their desks, pick up a pencil, and write their names. (visual, auditory, kinesthetic)

If you are left-handed . . .

Sit this way. It will be easier to write legibly because your body is well balanced.

Hold your pencil like this so you can be comfortable—even if you write for a long while.

Your paper should slant with the lower right corner pointing toward you. Then you can control your writing and make it slant the way you want it to.

44

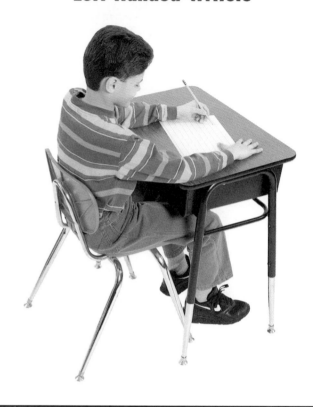

COACHING HINT: LEFT-HANDED WRITERS

You may wish to group left-handed students together for instruction if you can do so without calling attention to the practice. They should be seated to the left of the chalkboard.

PENCIL POSITION

PAPER POSITION

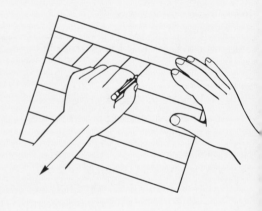

Right-Handed Writers

If you are right-handed . . .

Sit this way. It will be easier to write legibly because your body is well balanced.

Hold your pencil like this so you can be comfortable—even if you write for a long while.

Your paper should slant with the lower left corner pointing toward you. Then you can control your writing and make it slant the way you want it to.

45

COACHING HINT: USE OF THE CHALKBOARD

You and your students can follow these suggestions for writing on the chalkboard.

Left-handed writers. Stand in front of the writing lines and pull the downstrokes to the left elbow. The elbow is bent, and the writing is done at a comfortable height. Step to the right often to maintain correct slant.

Right-handed writers. Stand to the left of the writing lines and pull the downstrokes toward the midsection of the body. The elbow is bent, and the writing is done at a comfortable height. Step to the right often to maintain correct slant. (visual, kinesthetic)

EVALUATE

Check for correct paper and pencil position. The Zaner-Bloser Writing Frame can be used to help improve hand position.

PENCIL POSITION

PAPER POSITION

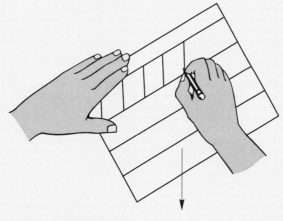

Students can use the chart on this page to identify lowercase cursive letters and numerals. (visual, auditory)

Practice Masters 87 and 89 are available for use with these pages.

Lowercase Cursive Letters and Numerals

a a   b b   c c   d d   e e   f f   g g
h h   i i   j j   k k   l l   m m   n n
o o   p p   q q   r r   s s   t t   u u
v v   w w   x x   y y   z z

1   2   3   4   5   6   7   8   9   10

Circle the lowercase cursive letters that are in your name.

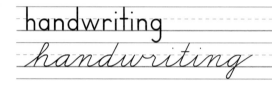

handwriting
handwriting

Look at these two words. How are they different?

46

COACHING HINT

Give half the students manuscript letter cards and the other half corresponding cursive letter cards. On a signal, have them scramble to locate their partners. Repeat several times to reinforce the identification of the cursive letters. (visual, kinesthetic)

Read the word written in cursive.
Circle the matching word written in manuscript.

dog   hog   boy   dog
lamb   lamb   lame   damp
bear   dear   bear   bean

Write each word in manuscript.

lion _____   *tiger* _____

pony _____   *pig* _____

47

EVALUATE

Poll students to find out which lowercase cursive letters and numerals are most difficult for them to read. Discuss possible reasons for this difficulty. Then ask students to describe the similarities and differences between the manuscript and cursive letters and numerals.

Ask students to describe the similarities and differences between the cursive writing they read and the manuscript writing they wrote.

Students can use the chart on this page to identify uppercase cursive letters and punctuation. (visual, auditory)

Practice Masters 87 and 89 are available for use with these pages.

Uppercase Cursive Letters

Aa Bb Cc Dd Ee Ff Gg
Hh Ii Jj Kk Ll Mm Nn
Oo Pp Qq Rr Ss Tt Uu
Vv Ww Xx Yy Zz !! ??

Circle the uppercase cursive letters that begin your first and last names.

Circle the uppercase cursive letter that begins the name of your school.

How are these sentences different?

Kelly lives in Dallas.

Kelly lives in Dallas.

48

COACHING HINT

Review with students the use of guidelines for correct letter formation. Draw guidelines on the chalkboard, using colored chalk to identify the headline, midline, and baseline. Invite volunteers to write words on the guidelines. (visual, auditory, kinesthetic)

Write each letter in manuscript.

C _____ E _____ I _____ O _____

U _____ B _____ D _____ F _____

G _____ K _____ Q _____ R _____

S _____ V _____ P _____ H _____

Write each name in manuscript.

Molly _____

Alaska _____

Tyrone _____

Zaire _____

49

UNDERCURVE
Touch the baseline; curve under and up to the midline.

UNDERCURVE
Touch the baseline; curve under and up to the headline.

DOWNCURVE
Touch the midline; curve left and down to the baseline.

DOWNCURVE
Touch the headline; curve left and down to the baseline.

50

Important Strokes for Cursive Writing

Undercurves swing.
Downcurves dive.
Overcurves bounce.
Slants just slide.

Undercurve
Write undercurve strokes.

Downcurve
Write downcurve strokes.

50

MODEL THE WRITING

Model the two sizes of each stroke on guidelines. Invite students to say the names as they write the strokes in the air. Point out that cursive letters are formed from these basic strokes. Don't write letters.

Undercurve, downcurve.
Overcurve, slant.
As you write cursive letters.
Remember this chant.

Overcurve
Write overcurve strokes.

Slant
Write slant strokes.

51

OVERCURVE
Touch the baseline; curve up and right to the midline.

OVERCURVE
Touch the baseline; curve up and right to the headline.

SLANT
Touch the midline; slant left to the baseline.

SLANT
Touch the headline; slant left to the baseline.

COACHING HINT

Provide sheets of newspaper and a dark crayon for each student. Let students tape their newspapers to a chalkboard or wall and practice their strokes in large, sweeping motions. Encourage them to practice each stroke several times and to feel the motion that each one involves. (kinesthetic, visual)

EVALUATE

To help students evaluate their writing, ask questions such as these:
Do your undercurve and overcurve strokes start at the baseline?
Do your downcurve strokes end at the baseline?
Are your slant strokes pulled toward the baseline?

Tell students that all letters of the same size should be even in height. Tall letters (those a full space high) touch the headline. Short letters (letters one-half space high) touch the midline. Letters with descenders extend below the baseline.

PRACTICE MASTERS FOR UNIT 4

Keys to Legibility: Size and Shape
Make your writing easy to read.

Let's look at the size and shape of lowercase cursive letters.

Tall letters touch the headline.

b d f k t

Short letters touch the midline.

a c n s x

Some letters go below the baseline.

f g j q z

Look at the letters below.
Circle the green letters that are the correct size and shape.

a n b p e q g r h

a n b p e q g r h

u i v k w l y m z

u i v k w l y m z

52

In this section students are introduced to three keys to legibility for cursive letters: size and shape of lowercase letters and slant. The lessons that follow emphasize lowercase letter formation and joinings. Students evaluate their work and circle their best letter in each lesson.

PREVIEW

Preview this section by calling attention to these features:
- letter models in both manuscript and cursive
- cursive letter models with numbered directional arrows
- guidelines for student writing directly beneath handwriting models
- opportunities to evaluate lowercase letter size and shape
- opportunities to evaluate slant
- a writing activity for manuscript maintenance
- review lessons of lowercase letters grouped by initial stroke

COACHING HINT: SIZE

Demonstrate for students the technique of drawing a horizontal line with a ruler along the tops of letters to show proper size. Have students come to the chalkboard and use colored chalk and a ruler to draw horizontal lines along the top of a group of tall letters and a group of short letters. Have students practice this technique periodically to evaluate their letter size. (kinesthetic, visual)

COACHING HINT: SHAPE

Review with students the use of the guidelines for correct letter formation. As you demonstrate on the chalkboard, have students do the following on paper:
- Draw over the baseline with a red crayon.
- Draw over the headline and midline with a blue crayon. (kinesthetic, visual, auditory)

Keys to Legibility: Slant

Cursive letters have a forward slant.

a b c d e f g h i j

POSITION
PULL
SHIFT

Check your paper position.
Pull your downstrokes in the right direction.
Shift your paper as you write.

If you are left-handed . . .

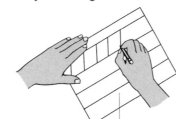

pull toward your left elbow.

If you are right-handed . . .

pull toward your midsection.

Check the slant.
Draw lines through the slant strokes in the letters.

uneven   good

53

COACHING HINT: SLANT

Practicing slant lines at the chalkboard is a good way to improve poor slant strokes. Have students use soft, oversize chalk, holding it as they would hold a pencil. You may want to begin by placing sets of two dots about six inches apart and at the correct slant to mark the starting and stopping points of each slant stroke. (kinesthetic, visual)

KEYS TO LEGIBILITY: SLANT

Tell students that in cursive writing all letters should have the same slant. On the chalkboard, show an example of cursive writing with correct slant. Use colored chalk to draw parallel lines through the slant strokes of the letters.

slant

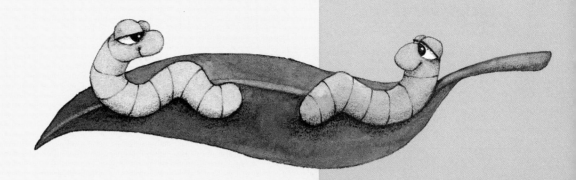

Undercurve
Slant, undercurve,
(lift)
Dot

COACHING HINT

Students' progress in handwriting is greater when short, intensive periods of instruction are used, approximately fifteen minutes for a lesson.

Note: In each Evaluate section, the letterforms illustrate common problems in letter formation.

Circle i and *i* in these words.

six insects singing
six insects singing

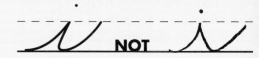

Trace and write.

Join *i* and *i*.

Circle your best *i*.

54

MODEL THE WRITING

Write **i** on guidelines as you say the stroke descriptions. To help students visualize the letter, model **i** in the air. Have students say the stroke descriptions as they write **i** in the air with you. Ask questions such as these:
What are the three strokes in **i**? *(undercurve, slant, undercurve)*
Where is the dot? *(halfway between the headline and the midline)*

EVALUATE

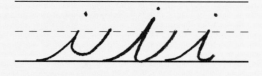

To help students evaluate their writing, ask questions such as these:
Does your letter rest on the baseline?
Does your first stroke end at the midline?
Does your last stroke end at the midline?

PRACTICE

Let students use laminated writing cards or slates to practice writing the letter.

CORRECTIVE STRATEGY

i **NOT** *i*

Pull the slant stroke toward the baseline and pause before making the undercurve ending.

Circle t and *t* in these words.

two turtles talking
two turtles talking

Trace and write.

t   t   t   t   t   t

Join *t* and other letters.

tt   tt   tt   ti   ti   ti

Write the word *it*.

it   it   it   it   it

Circle your best *t*

55

Undercurve
Slant, undercurve,
  (lift)
Slide right

Write Away

Provide sheets of newspaper and a dark crayon for each student. Let students tape their newspapers to a chalkboard or wall and practice their strokes in large, sweeping motions. Then have students use strokes to make pictures. (kinesthetic, visual)

PRACTICE MASTER 22

MODEL THE WRITING

Write **t** on guidelines as you say the stroke descriptions. To help students visualize the letter, model **t** in the air. Have students say the stroke descriptions as they write **t** in the air with you. Ask questions such as these:
Where does the first undercurve end? *(at the headline)*
Where does the second undercurve end? *(at the midline)*

EVALUATE

To help students evaluate their writing, ask questions such as these:
Is your slant stroke pulled toward the baseline?
Is your **t** crossed above the midline?
Does your first undercurve end at the headline?

PRACTICE

Let students use laminated writing cards or slates to practice writing the letter.

CORRECTIVE STRATEGY

it

NOT

it

Swing wide on the undercurve to undercurve joining.

Undercurve
Slant, undercurve
Slant, undercurve

COACHING HINT

Students can evaluate slant by drawing lines through the slant strokes of their letters. The lines should be parallel and should show the correct degree of forward slant. (visual)

PRACTICE MASTER 23

Circle u and *u* in these words.

four bunnies surfing
four bunnies surfing

Trace and write.

u *u*

Join *u* and other letters.

ut   tu   utu   uit

Write words with *u*.

tut   tut   tutu

Circle your best *u*.

MODEL THE WRITING

Write **u** on guidelines as you say the stroke descriptions. To help students visualize the letter, model **u** in the air. Have students say the stroke descriptions as they write **u** in the air with you. Ask questions such as these:
How many slant strokes are in **u**? *(two)*
How many undercurves are in **u**? *(three)*

EVALUATE

To help students evaluate their writing, ask questions such as these:
Does your **u** begin at the baseline?
Does your **u** end at the midline?
Is your **u** about the same width as the model?

PRACTICE

Let students use laminated writing cards or slates to practice writing the letter.

CORRECTIVE STRATEGY

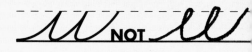

Pause before writing the slant strokes.

Circle w and *w* in these words.

twin worms waving
twin worms waving

Trace and write.

| w *w* | *w w w w w* |

Join *w* and other letters.

wi wu wt tw twi

Write the word *wit*.

wit wit wit

Circle your best *w*.

57

Undercurve
Slant, undercurve
Slant, undercurve
Checkstroke

Write **A**way

Ask students to develop a video or computer game. Have them design a label for it and write a word (in manuscript or cursive) that could be used to describe it. Ask them to use words with **w**. (visual)

MODEL THE WRITING

Write **w** on guidelines as you say the stroke descriptions. Have students say the stroke descriptions as they write **w** in the air with you. Ask questions such as these:
How is **w** like **u**? (*Both begin with an undercurve; both have slant strokes; both have three undercurves.*)
How is the last stroke in **w** different from the last stroke in **u**? (*The letter **w** ends with a checkstroke.*)

EVALUATE

W w

To help students evaluate their writing, ask questions such as these:
Are your slant strokes pulled down straight to the baseline?
Does your checkstroke begin and end at the midline?

PRACTICE

Let students use laminated writing cards or slates to practice writing the letter.

CORRECTIVE STRATEGY

wi

NOT

wi

In the checkstroke to undercurve joining, it is best to deepen the retrace a little before swinging into the undercurve of the next letter.

PRACTICE MASTER 24

Look at the large letter carefully. Make sure the paper is in the correct position. Trace the letter.

w w w w

Position the paper correctly. Write the letter and the joinings.

w w w w w w w

wi wu wt tw

Name

Copyright © Zaner-Bloser, Inc.   PRACTICE MASTER 24

Review the letters **i**, **t**, **u**, and **w** by writing them on the chalkboard. Ask questions such as these:
What is the same about all four letters? *(All begin with an undercurve.)*
Which letter ends differently from the others? *(w)*
How does it end? *(with a checkstroke)*
How do the others end? *(with an undercurve)*

Ask volunteers to call out various combinations of two of the four letters. Demonstrate the joining method for each pair. Emphasize the different stroke needed when **w** is the initial letter—checkstroke to undercurve.

Write Away

Ask students to imagine they have a pet insect, turtle, bunny, or worm. Have them write and illustrate a sentence about their imaginary pet. Participate by describing your own imaginary pet. *(visual, auditory, kinesthetic)*

Review

Write these letter joinings.

ti tu tw ui ut

wi wt wu twi

Circle your best joining.

Write these words.

it wit tutu

Do your short letters touch the midline?

58

COACHING HINT: LEFT-HANDED WRITERS

Seat left-handed students to the left side of the chalkboard.

EVALUATE

To help students evaluate their writing, ask questions such as these:
Is your **i** dotted?
Does your **t** touch the headline?
Are your joinings formed correctly?
Is your **wu** joining legible?

Circle r and _r_ in these words.

three roosters racing
three roosters racing

Trace and write.

r _r_   _r r r r r r_

Join _r_ and other letters.

_ri   rt   ir   ur   wr_

Write words with _r_.

rut   rut   writ

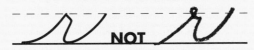

Circle your best _r_.

59

COACHING HINT

Draw writing lines on one side of 9" x 12" pieces of oak tag, and laminate one for each student. Students can use these as "slates" by practicing their handwriting with a wipe-off crayon. The reverse side can be used for such things as letter activities. (visual, kinesthetic)

MODEL THE WRITING

Write **r** on guidelines as you say the stroke descriptions. To help students visualize the letter, model **r** in the air. Have students say the stroke descriptions as they write **r** in the air with you. Ask questions such as these:
How does **r** begin? *(with an undercurve)*
What stroke follows the first undercurve? *(slant right)*
How does **r** end? *(with an undercurve)*

EVALUATE

To help students evaluate their writing, ask questions such as these:
Does your first undercurve end at the midline?
Does your **r** have correct slant?

PRACTICE

Let students use laminated writing cards or slates to practice writing the letter.

CORRECTIVE STRATEGY

_r_ **NOT** _r_

Pause after the first undercurve and slant right.

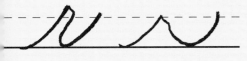

Look at the large letter carefully. Make sure the paper is in the correct position. Trace the letter.

Position the paper correctly. Write the letter and the joinings.

Name

59

**Undercurve
Retrace, curve down
and back
Undercurve**

COACHING HINT

Use the overhead projector
to project **s** onto the chalkboard. Ask students to wet
their index fingers in a cup
of water and to trace over
the letter on the chalkboard.
(kinesthetic, visual)

PRACTICE MASTER 26

Circle s and _s_ in these words.

six skunks swimming
six skunks swimming

Trace and write.

| s |

_s_   _s_   _s_   _s_   _s_

Join _s_ and other letters.

_si_   _st_   _sw_   _rs_   _ss_

Write words with _s_.

_us_   _its_   _sit_   _sir_

Circle your best _s_.

60

MODEL THE WRITING

Write **s** on guidelines as you say the stroke
descriptions. Have students say the stroke
descriptions as they write **s** in the air with
you. Ask questions such as these:
How is **s** like **r**? *(Both begin and end with
an undercurve.)*
How are they different? *(After the first
undercurve, **s** has a retrace followed by a
curve down and back; **r** has a slant right
stroke.)*

EVALUATE

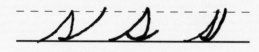

To help students evaluate their writing, ask
questions such as these:
Is the bottom of your **s** closed?
Does your **s** end at the midline?
Is your **s** about the same width as the
model?

PRACTICE

Let students use laminated writing cards or
slates to practice writing the letter.

CORRECTIVE STRATEGY

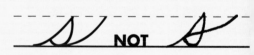

Be sure the final undercurve touches the
baseline.

Circle p and *p* in these words.

puppies pushing prams
puppies pushing prams

Trace and write.

| p | *p* |

p   p   p   p   p

Join *p* and other letters.

pi   pu   pr   rp   sp

Write words with *p*.

put pup up rips

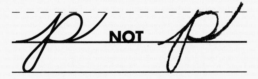

Circle your best *p*.

61

Undercurve
Slant, loop back
Overcurve, curve
  back
Undercurve

MODEL THE WRITING

Write **p** on guidelines as you say the stroke descriptions. To help students visualize the letter, model **p** in the air. Have students say the stroke descriptions as they write **p** in the air with you. Ask questions such as these:
Where does the beginning undercurve end? *(at the midline)*
Where does the loop close? *(near the baseline)*

EVALUATE

p   p   p

To help students evaluate their writing, ask questions such as these:
Does your beginning undercurve end at the midline?
Does your loop fill the descender space?
Does your slant loop to the left?

PRACTICE

Let students use laminated writing cards or slates to practice writing the letter.

CORRECTIVE STRATEGY

p **NOT** *p*

Close the loop near the baseline.

Write Away

Challenge students to write words using one or more of the letters **i**, **t**, **u**, **w**, **r**, **s**, and **p**. Some students may want to try using cursive letters, experimenting with letters they want to use but have not yet been taught. Others may prefer to use manuscript. (auditory, kinesthetic)

PRACTICE MASTER 27

**Undercurve
Slant
Loop back,
  overcurve, (lift)
Dot**

COACHING HINT

A good book to read to students who are just starting cursive writing is *Muggie Maggie* by Beverly Cleary. (auditory)

Circle j and ƒ in these words.

joeys juggling jars
joeys juggling jars

Trace and write.

j   *j j j j j*

Join ƒ and other letters.

ji   ju   jit   jur   jus

Write words with ƒ.

jut   juts   just

Circle your best ƒ.

62

MODEL THE WRITING

Write **j** on guidelines as you say the stroke descriptions. To help students visualize the letter, model **j** in the air. Have students write **j** in the air with you. Ask questions such as these:
Where does **j** begin? *(at the baseline)*
Where does the overcurve end? *(at the midline)*
Where is the dot? *(halfway between the headline and the midline)*

EVALUATE

To help students evaluate their writing, ask questions such as these:
Is your slant stroke pulled through the baseline?
Does your loop close at the baseline?
Does your **j** end with an overcurve?

PRACTICE

Let students use laminated writing cards or slates to practice writing the letter.

CORRECTIVE STRATEGY

NOT

In the overcurve to undercurve joining, the overcurve ending stops at the baseline to blend with the undercurve beginning.

Review

Write these letter joinings.

pr sp ju tr

Circle your best joining.

Write these words.

its sir tip up

stir just

Circle the word with the best slant.

63

COACHING HINT: LEFT-HANDED WRITERS

You might want to group left-handed students together for handwriting lessons.

EVALUATE

To help students evaluate their writing, ask questions such as these:
Are your joinings formed correctly?
Do **r, s, p,** and **j** touch the midline?
Do the descenders in **p** and **j** fill the descender space?

Review the letters **r, s, p,** and **j** by asking questions such as these:
How do all the letters begin? *(with an undercurve)*
Which of these letters ends differently? *(The j ends with an overcurve.)*
Which letters have a descender? *(p, j)*

Review the joining techniques by writing the following combinations on the chalkboard. Say the strokes as you write them.

ji   tr   uw   sp

st   wi   ju   wr

Have students write each combination three times on paper. Suggest they underline their best joining.

Write Away

Ask students to choose one of the animals shown at the top of page 63 and to write a sentence telling how it moves. Participate by telling whether one of these animals walks, runs, or jumps. (kinesthetic)

I can jump.

**Downcurve
Undercurve
Slant, undercurve**

COACHING HINT

As students continue the transition from manuscript to cursive, they may find that maintaining correct spacing between letters is difficult. The joining stroke between letters must be wide enough to allow for good spacing. The exercise below will reinforce both fluent strokes and good spacing. (visual, kinesthetic)

PRACTICE MASTER 29

Circle a and *a* in these words.

alpacas at play
alpacas at play

Trace and write.

a *a*   *a a a a a*

Join *a* and other letters.

ai   ap   ar   aw   ta

Write words with *a*.

artist   saw   start

Circle your best *a*.

64

MODEL THE WRITING

Write **a** on guidelines as you say the stroke descriptions. To help students visualize the letter, model **a** in the air. Have students say the stroke descriptions as they write **a** in the air with you. Ask questions such as these:
Where does the downcurve stroke begin? (*just below the midline*)
Where does **a** end? (*at the midline*)
Name the strokes in **a**. (*downcurve, undercurve, slant, undercurve*)

EVALUATE

a a

To help students evaluate their writing, ask questions such as these:
Is your **a** closed?
Does your **a** end at the midline?

PRACTICE

Let students use laminated writing cards or slates to practice writing the letter.

CORRECTIVE STRATEGY

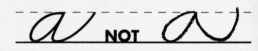

Pull the slant stroke correctly toward the baseline.

Circle c and _c_ in these words.

cool cows camping
cool cows camping

Trace and write.

_c c c c c c_

Join _c_ and other letters.

ca ci scr ct rc

Write words with _c_.

cup car act cut

Circle your best _c_.

65

**Downcurve
Undercurve**

Write Away

Challenge students to use the letters **t, w, r, s, p, j,** and **c** to write rhyming words for _wit, paw, sat, car,_ and _rut_ by substituting different letters for the initial letter. Some students may still prefer to use manuscript writing. Others may want to experiment with cursive writing. (auditory)

MODEL THE WRITING

Write **c** on guidelines as you say the stroke descriptions. To help students visualize the letter, model **c** in the air. Have students say the stroke descriptions as they write **c** in the air with you. Ask questions such as these:
Where does **c** begin? (below the midline)
How does **c** end? (with an undercurve)

EVALUATE

_c c c_

To help students evaluate their writing, ask questions such as these:
Does your **c** have correct slant?
Does your **c** begin below the midline?
Does your **c** end at the midline?

PRACTICE

Let students use laminated writing cards or slates to practice writing the letter.

CORRECTIVE STRATEGY

_ci_ NOT _ci_

Swing wide on the undercurve to undercurve joining.

PRACTICE MASTER 30

Trace and write
_c c c c c c_

Write
ci ca ct scr acr

cat crust circus

EVALUATE Circle your best joining. Circle your best word.

Name

Copyright © Zaner-Bloser, Inc.   PRACTICE MASTER 30

**Downcurve
Undercurve
Slant, undercurve**

COACHING HINT

Provide a shallow tray or box lid with a thin layer of sand in it. Allow students to form **d** and other letters in the sand. (kinesthetic)

PRACTICE MASTER 31

Circle d and *d* in these words.

dry ducks daydreaming
dry ducks daydreaming

Trace and write.

d *d*   *d d d d d*

Join *d* and other letters.

da   di   dr   du   id

Write words with *d*.

add   said   dirt

Circle your best *d*.

66

MODEL THE WRITING

Write **d** on guidelines as you say the stroke descriptions. To help students visualize the letter, model **d** in the air. Have students say the stroke descriptions as they write **d** in the air with you. Ask questions such as these:
Where does **d** begin? *(just below the midline)*
Where does **d** end? *(at the midline)*
How does **d** begin? *(with a downcurve)*
How does **d** end? *(with an undercurve)*

EVALUATE

d d

To help students evaluate their writing, ask questions such as these:
Does your first undercurve end at the headline?
Does your **d** end at the midline?

PRACTICE

Let students use laminated writing cards or slates to practice writing the letter.

CORRECTIVE STRATEGY

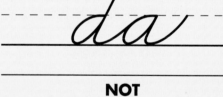

NOT

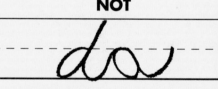

The undercurve to downcurve joining becomes a doublecurve.

66

Circle q and *q* in these words.

squirrels squirting
squirrels squirting

Trace and write.

q q q q q

Join *q* and other letters.

qu qui aqu squ

Write words with *q*.

quit quart aqua

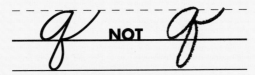

Circle your best *q*.

**Downcurve
Undercurve
Slant
Loop forward,
undercurve**

COACHING HINT

To stress correct joining strokes, ask the students to write a word in cursive on the chalkboard and to use colored chalk to highlight the joining strokes. (visual)

MODEL THE WRITING

Write **q** on guidelines as you say the stroke descriptions. To help students visualize the letter, have them write **q** in the air with you. Ask questions such as these:
How does **q** begin? *(with a downcurve)*
How does **q** end? *(with an undercurve)*
Where does the loop in **q** close? *(at the baseline)*

EVALUATE

q q q

To help students evaluate their writing, ask questions such as these:
Does your **q** have correct slant?
Does your loop close at the baseline?
Does your loop fill the descender space?

PRACTICE

Let students use laminated writing cards or slates to practice writing the letter.

CORRECTIVE STRATEGY

q NOT *q*

Close the loop at the baseline.

PRACTICE MASTER 32

Trace and write
q q q q q q q

Write
qu qua quu squ

quarts squirts

EVALUATE Circle your best joining. Circle your best word.

Name

Copyright © Zaner-Bloser, Inc.   PRACTICE MASTER 32

Downcurve
Undercurve
Slant
Loop back, overcurve

COACHING HINT

Correct body position is important. Encourage students to sit comfortably erect, with their feet flat on the floor and their hips touching the back of the chair. Both arms rest on the desk. The elbows are off the desk. Tell students they will be able to write more easily and for a longer time if they sit in a good writing position. (kinesthetic)

PRACTICE MASTER 33

Circle g and *g* in these words.

eight goats digging
eight goats digging

Trace and write.

g *g*   *g g g g g*

Join *g* and other letters.

ga   gi   gu   gr   ag

Write words with *g*.

gas   rug   grass

Circle your best *g*

68

MODEL THE WRITING

Write **g** on guidelines as you say the stroke descriptions. To help students visualize the letter, model **g** in the air. Have students say the stroke descriptions as they write **g** in the air with you. Ask questions such as these:

How does **g** differ from **q**? *(The letter **g** loops back and ends with an overcurve; **q** loops forward and ends with an undercurve.)*

Where does the loop in **g** close? *(at the baseline)*

EVALUATE

To help students evaluate their writing, ask questions such as these:
Is your letter closed at the top?
Does your loop close at the baseline?

PRACTICE

Let students use laminated writing cards or slates to practice writing the letter.

CORRECTIVE STRATEGY

ga

NOT

ga

In the overcurve to downcurve joining, the overcurve ends at the beginning of the downcurve.

Circle o and *o* in these words.

one octopus rowing
one octopus rowing

Trace and write.

o o

o o o o o o o

Join *o* and other letters.

oa oo oi ou wo

Write words with *o*.

two grow road

Circle your best *o*.

69

MODEL THE WRITING

Write **o** on guidelines as you say the stroke descriptions. To help students visualize the letter, model **o** in the air. Have students say the stroke descriptions as they write **o** in the air with you. Ask questions such as these:
Where does **o** begin? *(just below the midline)*
Where does **o** end? *(at the midline)*
What strokes are in **o**? *(downcurve, undercurve, checkstroke)*

EVALUATE

o o o

To help students evaluate their writing, ask questions such as these:
Does your **o** begin below the midline?
Is your oval closed?
Does your checkstroke end at the midline?

PRACTICE

Let students use laminated writing cards or slates to practice writing the letter.

CORRECTIVE STRATEGY

oa

NOT

oa

The checkstroke to downcurve joining swings much wider than the checkstroke to undercurve joining because of the downcurve.

Downcurve
Undercurve
Checkstroke

Write Away

Challenge students to use some of the letters **i, t, u, w, r, s, p, j, a, c, d, q, g,** and **o** to form new words by changing one letter in each of these words: *pit, car, jog, sad, cow.* Encourage students to write in both cursive and manuscript forms. **(auditory)**

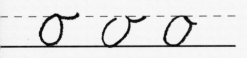

Review the letters **a, c, d, q, g,** and **o** by writing them on the chalkboard and saying the stroke descriptions with students. Ask a volunteer to demonstrate the correct formation of each letter. Have volunteers give the class clues that describe one of these letters, for example:

• This letter has a loop forward descender. **(q)**
• This letter touches the headline. **(d)**
• This letter ends with a checkstroke. **(o)**

Challenge the other students to identify the letter described. Encourage the volunteers to use correct terms in their clues.

Write Away

Ask students to choose one of the animals shown at the top of page 70 and to write a sentence telling why they would like to be that animal. Participate by telling which of these animals you would like to be and why. (auditory)

Review

Write these words.

saw   dad   cup   road

quart   grass   drop

Circle your best word.

Write this phrase.

two sad cats

Do *q* and *g* go below the baseline?

70

COACHING HINT

Remind students that a little more space is needed before a word that begins with a downcurve letter (**a, c, d, g, o,** and **q**). Write on the chalkboard a sentence such as *An alligator gave the ducks quite a scare.* Use colored chalk to indicate the space needed. (visual)

EVALUATE

To help students evaluate their writing, ask questions such as these:
Are your downcurve letters written correctly?
Are your checkstroke joinings written correctly?
Are the size and shape of your letters satisfactory?

Circle n and *n* in these words.

nine newts running

nine newts running

Trace and write.

n *n*

n n n n n

Join *n* and other letters.

na ni nn nt ing

Write words with *n*.

no running rain

Circle your best *n*.

71

Overcurve, slant
Overcurve, slant
Undercurve

COACHING HINT

Writing rate will increase as students begin to move the writing hand more freely. Have students practice writing letters and words in large size with crayon on folded newsprint to overcome finger motion. (kinesthetic)

PRACTICE MASTER 35

Trace and write.

Write.

EVALUATE Circle your best joining. Circle your best word.

Name

Copyright © Zaner-Bloser, Inc.   PRACTICE MASTER 35

MODEL THE WRITING

Write **n** on guidelines as you say the stroke descriptions. Have students say the stroke descriptions as they write **n** in the air with you. Ask questions such as these:
How does **n** begin? *(with an overcurve)*
How does **n** end? *(with an undercurve)*
How many overcurves are in **n**? *(two)*
How many slant strokes are in **n**? *(two)*

EVALUATE

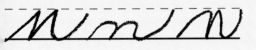

To help students evaluate their writing, ask questions such as these:
Are your overcurves round?
Do your overcurves touch the midline?
Does your **n** have correct slant?

PRACTICE

Let students use laminated writing cards or slates to practice writing the letter.

CORRECTIVE STRATEGY

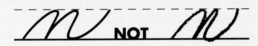 **NOT**

Make sure there is enough space between the overcurves.

71

Overcurve, slant
Overcurve, slant
Overcurve, slant
Undercurve

COACHING HINT: LEFT-HANDED WRITERS

Right-handed teachers will better understand the stroke, vision, and posture of the left-handed student if they practice the left-handed position themselves. The Zaner-Bloser Writing Frame can help students achieve correct hand position, because the hand holding the pencil and resting over the frame automatically settles into the correct position. (kinesthetic)

PRACTICE MASTER 36

Circle m and *m* in these words.

many mice marching
many mice marching

Trace and write.

m m m m m

Join *m* and other letters.

ma mi mm mo rm

Write words with *m*.

mom jump coming

Circle your best *m*.

72

MODEL THE WRITING

Write **m** on guidelines as you say the stroke descriptions. To help students visualize the letter, model **m** in the air. Have students say the stroke descriptions as they write **m** in the air with you. Ask questions such as these:
How many overcurves are in **m**? *(three)*
How many slant strokes are in **m**? *(three)*
How many times does **m** touch the midline? *(four)*

EVALUATE

To help students evaluate their writing, ask questions such as these:
Is there enough space between your overcurves?
Does your **m** rest on the baseline?

PRACTICE

Let students use laminated writing cards or slates to practice writing the letter.

CORRECTIVE STRATEGY

NOT

The undercurve to overcurve joining becomes a doublecurve. The doublecurve becomes a part of the following letter.

72

Circle x and *x* in these words.

six foxes fox-trotting
six foxes fox-trotting

Trace and write.

x   x   x   x   x   x

Join *x* and other letters.

xa   xi   ix   xt   ixt

Write words with *x*.

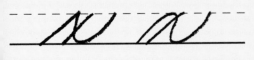

ax   ox   taxi   six

Circle your best *x*.

73

Overcurve, slant
Undercurve, (lift)
Slant

Write Away

Challenge students to form real words by using the letters **i, t, u, w, r, s, p, j, a, c, d, q, g, o, n, m,** and **x** to fill in the blanks of these words. (auditory)

_it	_ing	m_n
d_g	_oon	_ax
a_t	p_rt	cu_
j_r	st_r	m_x
qui_		

MODEL THE WRITING

Write **x** on guidelines as you say the stroke descriptions. Model **x** in the air. Have students say the stroke descriptions as they write **x** in the air with you. Ask questions such as these:
How does **x** begin? *(with an overcurve)*
Where does the overcurve end? *(at the midline)*
Where does the last slant stroke begin? *(at the midline)*
Where does the last slant stroke end? *(at the baseline)*

EVALUATE

To help students evaluate their writing, ask questions such as these:
Does your **x** have a good overcurve?
Is your **x** crossed in the middle of the first slant stroke?

PRACTICE

Let students use laminated writing cards or slates to practice writing the letter.

CORRECTIVE STRATEGY

x **NOT** *x*

After writing the overcurve, be sure to slant left toward the baseline.

PRACTICE MASTER 37

**Overcurve, slant
Undercurve
Slant
Loop back, overcurve**

COACHING HINT

Give half the students manuscript letter cards and the other half corresponding cursive letter cards. On a signal, have them scramble to locate their partners. Repeat several times to reinforce identification of the cursive letters. (visual, kinesthetic)

Circle y and *y* in these words.

young yaks yodeling
young yaks yodeling

Trace and write.

y *y*   *y   y   y   y   y*

Join *y* and other letters.

ya   ys   ay   oy   ty

Write words with *y*.

toys   crayon   your

Circle your best *y*

MODEL THE WRITING

Write **y** on guidelines as you say the stroke descriptions. To help students visualize the letter, model **y** in the air. Have students say the stroke descriptions as they write **y** in the air with you. Ask questions such as these:
How does **y** end? *(with an overcurve)*
How many overcurves are in **y**? *(two)*

EVALUATE

y y y

To help students evaluate their writing, ask questions such as these:
Does your loop close at the baseline?
Are your slant strokes pulled toward the baseline?
Does your **y** end with an overcurve at the midline?

PRACTICE

Let students use laminated writing cards or slates to practice writing the letter.

CORRECTIVE STRATEGY

y **NOT** *y*

Be sure the overcurve ending crosses the slant stroke at the baseline.

Circle z and *z* in these words.

zebras zigzagging
zebras zigzagging

Trace and write.

z *z*   *z z z z z*

Join *z* and other letters.

za   zi   zy   zz   iz

Write words with *z*.

zip   zoom   dizzy

Circle your best *z*.

75

Overcurve, slant
Overcurve
Curve down
Loop, overcurve

Write Away

Challenge students to write at least ten words using the letters **i, t, u, w, r, s, p, j, a, c, d, q, g, o, n, m, x, y,** and **z.** (visual, auditory)

MODEL THE WRITING

Write **z** on guidelines as you say the stroke descriptions. Have students say the stroke descriptions as they write **z** in the air with you. Ask questions such as these: How is the beginning stroke like the ending stroke? (*Both are overcurves.*) Where does the overcurve ending stop? (*at the midline*) Where does the loop close? (*at the baseline*)

EVALUATE

To help students evaluate their writing, ask questions such as these:
Does your loop close at the baseline?
Is your slant stroke pulled toward the baseline?
Does your loop fill the descender space?

PRACTICE

Let students use laminated writing cards or slates to practice writing the letter.

CORRECTIVE STRATEGY

z **NOT** *z*

Close the loop at the baseline.

PRACTICE MASTER 39

Trace and write
Write
EVALUATE Circle your best joining. Circle your best word.
Name

**Overcurve, slant
Undercurve
Checkstroke**

COACHING HINT

Most errors in slant can be corrected in one of the following ways:
1. Check paper position.
2. Be sure to pull the slant strokes in the proper direction.
3. Remember to shift the paper as the writing progresses across the line.

PRACTICE MASTER 40

Circle v and ν in these words.

seven vultures diving
seven vultures diving

Trace and write.

V ν

Join ν and other letters.

νa νi νo $a \nu$ $i \nu$ νy

Write words with ν.

νan $giving$ $wavy$

Circle your best ν.

76

MODEL THE WRITING

Write **v** on guidelines as you say the stroke descriptions. To help students visualize the letter, model **v** in the air. Have students say the stroke descriptions as they write **v** in the air with you. Ask questions such as these:
How does **v** end? *(with a checkstroke)*
What strokes are in **v**? *(overcurve, slant, undercurve, checkstroke)*

EVALUATE

To help students evaluate their writing, ask questions such as these:
Does your **v** end with a checkstroke?
Does your **v** have a good slant stroke?
Is your **v** about the same width as the model?

PRACTICE

Let students use laminated writing cards or slates to practice writing the letter.

CORRECTIVE STRATEGY

ν **NOT** ν

The overcurve stroke curves up and over.

Review

Write these words.

going   most   story

mix   zoo   giving

Circle your best word.

Write this phrase.

six gray vans

Do your ending strokes touch the midline?

77

COACHING HINT

On the chalkboard, demonstrate the letters with descenders. Have students trace each descender with colored chalk to highlight its shape and size. (kinesthetic, visual)

EVALUATE

To help students evaluate their writing, ask questions such as these:
Are your letters formed correctly?
Are your beginning overcurves rounded?

REFOCUS

Review the letters **n**, **m**, **x**, **y**, **z**, and **v**. Ask a volunteer to demonstrate the correct formation of each letter on the chalkboard. Encourage the student to describe the strokes used. Ask each student to write these letters on six cards or pieces of paper. Have students hold up a card that fits each of the following descriptions:
- This letter has no descender. *(n, m, x, v)*
- This letter begins at the baseline. *(n, m, x, y, z, v)*
- This letter has a lift. *(x)*
- This letter crosses itself at the baseline. *(y, z)*
- This letter uses an undercurve to join with the next letter. *(n, m, x)*

Write Away

Ask students to write a sentence about a newt, a mouse, a fox, a yak, a zebra, or a vulture. Participate by telling a fact about one of these animals. (kinesthetic)

Undercurve
Loop back, slant
Undercurve

COACHING HINT

Keep a record of the letters with which students are having problems. Give students writing exercises such as word lists and tongue twisters that will give them practice with these letters. (visual, kinesthetic)

PRACTICE MASTER 41

Circle e and *e* in these words.

ten eagles exercising
ten eagles exercising

Trace and write.

| e *e* |

e e e e e e

Join *e* and other letters.

ea en er et ie se

Write words with *e*.

end eat needed

Circle your best *e*.

78

MODEL THE WRITING

Write **e** on guidelines as you say the stroke descriptions. To help students visualize the letter, model **e** in the air. Have students say the stroke descriptions as they write **e** in the air with you. Ask questions such as these:
How does **e** begin? *(with an undercurve)*
Is **e** tall or short? *(short)*

EVALUATE

e e e

To help students evaluate their writing, ask questions such as these:
Are your lines not too light or too dark?
Does your **e** have a good loop?
Does your **e** end at the midline?

PRACTICE

Let students use laminated writing cards or slates to practice writing the letter.

CORRECTIVE STRATEGY

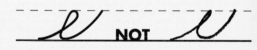

e **NOT** *u*

Be sure there is a loop in the letter.

Circle l and *l* in these words.

lemurs pulling tails
lemurs pulling tails

Trace and write.

l *l* *l* *l* *l*

Join *l* and other letters.

la *li* *le* *lo* *al* *ll*

Write words with *l*.

land *little* *call*

Circle your best *l*.

79

Undercurve
Loop back, slant
Undercurve

COACHING HINT

Continue to use the chalk-board for teaching the basic strokes, letters, joinings, and numerals. Students having motor-skill difficulty when they write on lined paper may benefit from the increased spacing the chalk-board provides. Since eras-ing is easy, identification and correction of errors becomes a simpler task. (kinesthetic, visual)

MODEL THE WRITING

Write l on guidelines as you say the stroke descriptions. Model l in the air. Have students say the stroke descriptions as they write l in the air with you. Ask questions such as these:
How are **e** and **l** different? *(The letter e is short; l is tall.)*
Where does the loop close in l? *(near the midline)*
What strokes are in both **e** and **l**? *(under-curve, loop back, slant, undercurve)*

EVALUATE

l *l* *l*

To help students evaluate their writing, ask questions such as these:
Does your loop close near the midline?
Does your l have correct slant?
Does your l touch the headline?

PRACTICE

Let students use laminated writing cards or slates to practice writing the letter.

CORRECTIVE STRATEGY

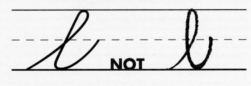

l **NOT** *l*

Pull the slant stroke straight toward the midsection (right-handers) or toward the left elbow (left-handers).

**Undercurve
Loop back, slant
Overcurve, slant
Undercurve**

COACHING HINT

On the chalkboard, write a line of lowercase letters with several obvious errors. Ask students to come to the chalkboard to locate, identify, and correct the errors. (visual, kinesthetic)

Circle h and *h* in these words.

three horses hiding

three horses hiding

Trace and write.

h   *h h h h h*

Join *h* and other letters.

ha   hea   ho   sh   th

Write words with *h*.

inch   hour   child

Circle your best *h*.

80

PRACTICE MASTER 43

Trace and write.
h h h h h h h

Write.
hi he has ch thy

hand house three

EVALUATE Circle your best joining. Circle your best word.

Name

Copyright © Zaner-Bloser, Inc.   PRACTICE MASTER 43

MODEL THE WRITING

Write **h** on guidelines as you say the stroke descriptions. To help students visualize the letter, model **h** in the air. Have students say the stroke descriptions as they write **h** in the air with you. Ask questions such as these:
What stroke follows the first slant? *(overcurve)*
How does **h** end? *(with an undercurve)*

EVALUATE

To help students evaluate their writing, ask questions such as these:
Is your **h** about the same width as the model?
Does your loop close near the midline?
Does your overcurve touch the midline?

PRACTICE

Let students use laminated writing cards or slates to practice writing the letter.

CORRECTIVE STRATEGY

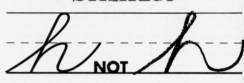

Close the loop near the midline and keep slant strokes parallel.

Circle k and *k* in these words.

koalas kayaking
koalas kayaking

k | *k*

Trace and write.

k k k k k

Join *k* and other letters.

ka ki ke cks sk

Write words with *k*.

know sky asked

Circle your best *k*.

81

Undercurve
Loop back, slant
Overcurve, curve
  forward, curve
  under
Slant right,
  undercurve

COACHING HINT
Have students form letters and joinings in a thin layer of finger paint spread on aluminum foil. (kinesthetic)

MODEL THE WRITING

Write **k** on guidelines as you say the stroke descriptions. To help students visualize the letter, model **k** in the air. Have students say the stroke descriptions as they write **k** in the air with you. Ask questions such as these:
How are **h** and **k** alike? *(Both begin and end with an undercurve; both have a loop that closes near the midline.)*
How many pauses are in **k**? *(two)*

EVALUATE

To help students evaluate their writing, ask questions such as these:
Is your **k** about the same width as the model?
Does your loop close near the midline?
Does your overcurve touch the midline?

PRACTICE

Let students use laminated writing cards or slates to practice writing the letter.

CORRECTIVE STRATEGY

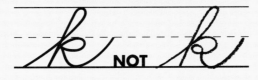

The curve under stroke is followed by a pause, slant right, and undercurve.

Trace and write
k k k k k k
Write
ku ki kno rk eak
kiss knee thank
EVALUATE Circle your best joining. Circle your best word.
Name

**Undercurve
Loop back, slant
Loop forward
Undercurve**

COACHING HINT

Holding the writing instrument correctly has an obvious effect on handwriting quality. Students having difficulty with the conventional method of holding the writing instrument may wish to try the alternate method of placing the pen or pencil between the first and second fingers. (kinesthetic)

PRACTICE MASTER 45

Circle f and *f* in these words.

five frogs fishing
five frogs fishing

Trace and write.

Join *f* and other letters.

Write words with *f*.

fold   off   after

Circle your best *f*.

82

MODEL THE WRITING

Write **f** on guidelines as you say the stroke descriptions. To help students visualize the letter, model **f** in the air. Have students say the stroke descriptions as they write **f** in the air with you. Ask questions such as these: How does **f** begin and end? *(with an undercurve)*
Where does the upper loop close? *(near the midline)*

EVALUATE

To help students evaluate their writing, ask questions such as these:
Does your **f** begin and end with an undercurve?
Does your upper loop close near the midline?
Does your lower loop close at the baseline?

PRACTICE

Let students use laminated writing cards or slates to practice writing the letter.

CORRECTIVE STRATEGY

NOT

Close the lower loop at the baseline.

Circle b and *b* in these words.

baby beavers bowling
baby beavers bowling

b *b*

Trace and write.

b b b b b

Join *b* and other letters.

ba bea bo by ab bb

Write words with *b*.

buy baby boxes

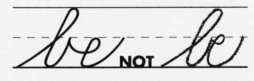

Circle your best *b*.

83

MODEL THE WRITING

Write **b** on guidelines as you say the stroke descriptions. Model **b** in the air. Have students say the stroke descriptions as they write **b** in the air with you. Ask questions such as these:

Where does the loop close in **b**? *(near the midline)*

Where does the second undercurve end? *(at the midline)*

How does **b** differ from **l**? *(The letter b ends with a checkstroke.)*

EVALUATE

b b b

To help students evaluate their writing, ask questions such as these:

Does your loop close near the midline?

Does your second undercurve end at the midline?

Does your checkstroke end at the midline?

PRACTICE

Let students use laminated writing cards or slates to practice writing the letter.

CORRECTIVE STRATEGY

be **NOT** *le*

In the checkstroke to undercurve joining, deepen the checkstroke a little before swinging into the undercurve of the next letter.

Write Away

Challenge students to write as many two-letter and three-letter words as they can using the 26 lowercase letters. You may want to set a time limit. If students are having difficulty, write the letters on the chalkboard. (visual, auditory)

PRACTICE MASTER 46

Trace and write.
b b b b b b

Write:
bu by bac blu ib
baseball bus job

EVALUATE Circle your best joining. Circle your best word.

Name

Review the letters **e**, **l**, **h**, **k**, **f**, and **b** by writing them on the chalkboard as you say the stroke descriptions. Review the undercurve to undercurve and checkstroke to undercurve joinings. Have volunteers write the following combinations on the chalkboard:

le	hi	lk	be
bi	fr	es	bl

Encourage students to describe both the strokes and the joinings as they form them, using the correct terms.

Write Away

Ask students to list the animals shown at the top of page 84 and to write the type of covering each one has.

Review

Write these words.

help   clean   bath

rock   fly   been

Circle your best word.

Write this phrase.

a funny joke

Do your tall letters touch the headline?

84

EVALUATE

To help students evaluate their writing, ask questions such as these:
Do all your letters end at the midline?
Do your tall letters touch the headline?
Does your **b** end with a checkstroke?

Review Lowercase Letters

Write these lowercase letters in cursive.

t p r w

s u j i

c a d o g q

n m v x y z

l b e k f h

Write these words in cursive.

hide

job

what

aunt

85

REFOCUS

Tell students they now have studied and written all the lowercase letterforms. Guide them in a review of these letters with the following activity.

1. The letters **t, w, p, r, i, j, s, u, b, k, h, f, e,** and **l** begin with the _____ stroke. *(undercurve)*
2. The letters **c, o, a, g, d,** and **q** begin with the _____ stroke. *(downcurve)*
3. The letters that begin with the overcurve stroke are _____. *(m, n, x, v, z, y)*
4. The letters **f, g, j, p, q, y,** and **z** have a _____. *(descender)*
5. The letters **b, o, v,** and **w** end with a _____. *(checkstroke)*

Have students review and practice the basic cursive strokes.

Remind students they have studied and written the lowercase cursive letters grouped according to beginning strokes. Write the cursive lowercase alphabet on the chalkboard and guide students in choosing the letters that complete each category of the following chart.

undercurve ending letters (a, c, d, e, f, h, i, k, l, m, n, p, q, r, s, t, u, x)	undercurve beginning letters (i, t, u, w, r, s, p, j, e, l, h, k, f, b)
overcurve ending letters (g, j, y, z)	downcurve beginning letters (a, c, d, q, g, o)
checkstroke ending letters (b, o, v, w)	overcurve beginning letters (n, m, x, y, z, v)

Tell students that joinings are formed by placing any letter from one column with a letter from the other column. If we choose the letter **a** from the left column and write it with the letter **i** from the right column, we have joined an undercurve-ending letter with an undercurve-beginning letter to form the undercurve to undercurve joining **ai**.

Have students write examples of each joining on the chalkboard.

COACHING HINT

To stress correct joining strokes, ask a volunteer to write a word on the chalkboard. Then have a second volunteer use colored chalk to highlight the joining strokes. (visual, kinesthetic)

EVALUATE

To help students evaluate their writing, ask questions such as these:
Are your letters and joinings formed correctly?
Do your tall letters touch the headline?
Do your short letters touch the midline?
Do your letters with descenders fill the descender space?

Review with students the size and shape of manuscript letters by demonstrating the four kinds of lines that are used in writing manuscript letters. Provide opportunities to practice the formation of each manuscript letter.

Remind students that manuscript writing is straight up and down. Demonstrate correct paper position and emphasize the direction in which to pull the strokes in order to write vertical lines.

Show an example of correct spacing between letters, words, and sentences. Remind students that letters and words that are too close together or too far apart make writing difficult to read. Provide opportunities to practice good spacing of letters and words on the handwriting guidelines.

Manuscript Maintenance

Write these tongue twisters in your best manuscript writing.

Sue sells small seashells.

Four flies flew far.

Many men marched.

Write a tongue twister of your own.

86

COACHING HINT

You may wish to have students do the following activities for reinforcement of manuscript writing.
1. Label pictures and objects.
2. Write the names of friends and pets.
3. Prepare invitations to parties.
4. List games for parties.
5. Send holiday greetings to parents and friends.
6. Write about excursions to centers of interest in the community.

EVALUATE

To help students evaluate their writing, ask questions such as these:
Are your backward and forward circles round?
Do your letters with pull down straight strokes stand up straight?
Do your short letters touch the midline?
Do your tall letters touch the headline?
Is your spacing between letters and words correct?

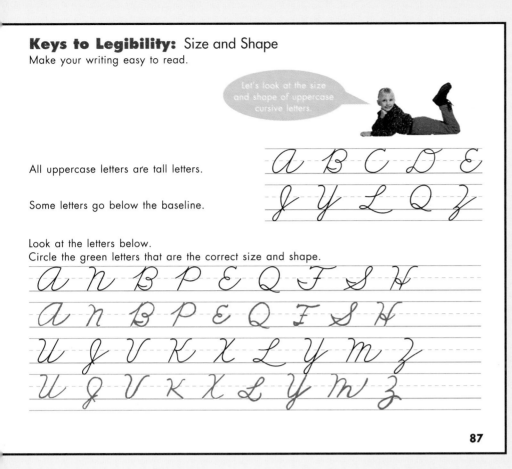

Keys to Legibility: Size and Shape

Make your writing easy to read.

Let's look at the size and shape of uppercase cursive letters.

All uppercase letters are tall letters.

Some letters go below the baseline.

Look at the letters below.
Circle the green letters that are the correct size and shape.

87

In this section students are introduced to the remaining keys to legibility for cursive letters: size and shape of uppercase letters and spacing. The lessons that follow emphasize uppercase letter formation and joinings and provide opportunities for writing uppercase letters in different contexts. Students evaluate their work and circle their best uppercase letter in each lesson.

PREVIEW

Preview this section by calling attention to these features:

• letter models in both manuscript and cursive
• cursive letter models with numbered directional arrows
• guidelines for student writing directly beneath handwriting models
• hints about joining uppercase letters to the letter that follows
• opportunities to evaluate uppercase letter size and shape
• opportunities to evaluate letter and word spacing
• a cursive numerals lesson
• review lessons of uppercase letters grouped by initial stroke

COACHING HINT: SIZE

Demonstrate for students the technique of drawing a horizontal line with a ruler along the tops of letters to show proper size. Have students come to the chalkboard and use colored chalk and a ruler to draw a horizontal line along the top of a group of uppercase letters. Have students practice this technique periodically to evaluate their letter size. (kinesthetic, visual)

COACHING HINT: SHAPE

Review with students the use of the guidelines for correct letter formation. As you demonstrate on the chalkboard, have students do the following on paper:

• Draw over the baseline with a red crayon.
• Draw over the headline and midline with a blue crayon. (kinesthetic, visual, auditory)

KEYS TO LEGIBILITY: SIZE AND SHAPE

Tell students that all uppercase letters are tall letters that touch the headline. Some uppercase letters go below the baseline.

PRACTICE MASTERS FOR UNIT 5

• Uppercase Cursive Letters, 47–72
• Cursive Numerals, 73
• Certificates, 75–77
• Letter to Parents—English, 84
• Letter to Parents—Spanish, 85
• Cursive Alphabet—English, 87
• Cursive Alphabet—Spanish, 89
• Cursive Stroke Descriptions—English, 98–100
• Cursive Stroke Descriptions—Spanish, 101–103
• Record of Student's Handwriting Skills, 74
• Zaner-Bloser Handwriting Grid, 126

Tell students that in cursive writing correct spacing is an important key to legible handwriting. There should be just enough space for a small oval between letters. Between words, the beginning stroke of one word should start near the ending stroke of the preceding word. A slanted line drawn from the endpoint of the last stroke to the baseline should touch both words. Show on the chalkboard an example of cursive writing with correct spacing. Use colored chalk to draw ovals and slanted lines.

Keys to Legibility: Spacing

This spacing is just right.

spacing between letters
spacing between words

Is there space for *o* between letters?

Circle the word in which the letter spacing is just right.

spacing   spacing

Is there space for ＼ between words?

Circle the sentence in which the word spacing is just right.

Is this easy to read?
Is this easy to read?
Is this easy to read?

COACHING HINT: SPACING

Remind students to shift their papers as they write to keep spacing consistent. (kinesthetic)

Circle A and a in these words.

All of us play together.

All of us play together.

Trace and write.

A a

a a a a a

a is joined to the letter that follows. Write words that begin with a.

April August Adam

Write a sentence that begins with a.

Anyone can win.

Circle your best a.

89

Downcurve
Undercurve
Slant, undercurve

Ask students to write a sentence about typical April or August weather conditions. (kinesthetic)

April is cool.

PRACTICE MASTER 47

Trace and write
a a a a a a

Write
Austria America

Atlanta is big.

EVALUATE Circle your best · Circle your best word

Name

Copyright © Zaner-Bloser, Inc.   PRACTICE MASTER 47

MODEL THE WRITING

Write **A** on guidelines as you say the stroke descriptions. To help students visualize the letter, model **A** in the air. Have students say the stroke descriptions as they write **A** in the air with you. Ask questions such as these:
How many strokes are in **A**? *(four)*
What are they? *(downcurve, undercurve, slant, undercurve)*

EVALUATE

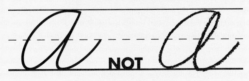

To help students evaluate their writing, ask questions such as these:
Is your **A** closed?
Does your **A** end at the midline?
Is your slant stroke pulled correctly toward the baseline?

PRACTICE

Let students use laminated writing cards or slates to practice writing the letter.

CORRECTIVE STRATEGY

a **NOT** $\mathcal{A}$

Pause before writing the slant stroke.

89

**Slant
Downcurve
Undercurve**

COACHING HINT

Write each student's name on a self-adhesive ruled name strip. Laminate it if you wish. Place the name strip on the student's desk to serve as a permanent model. (visual)

PRACTICE MASTER 48

Circle C and C in these words.

Can you come out to play?

Can you come out to play?

Trace and write.

C C   C C C C C

C is joined to the letter that follows. Write words that begin with C.

Cindy   Colorado   Carlos

Write a sentence that begins with C.

Cam plays ball.

Circle your best C.

90

MODEL THE WRITING

Write **C** on guidelines as you say the stroke descriptions. To help students visualize the letter, model **C** in the air. Have students say the stroke descriptions as they write **C** in the air with you. Ask questions such as these:
How does **C** begin? *(with a slant)*
What follows the slant? *(downcurve)*

EVALUATE

To help students evaluate their writing, ask questions such as these:
Does your **C** have correct slant?
Does your **C** begin with a slant stroke?
Does your **C** end at the midline?

PRACTICE

Let students use laminated writing cards or slates to practice writing the letter.

CORRECTIVE STRATEGY

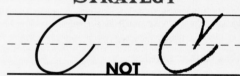

NOT

The first stroke is a short slant that begins at the headline.

Circle E and *E* in these words.

Everyone watched the parade.

Everyone watched the parade.

Trace and write.

E *E*   *E   E   E   E   E*

E is joined to the letter that follows. Write words that begin with *E*.

Europe   Eduardo   Elena

Write a sentence that begins with *E*.

Eli saw floats.

Circle your best *E*

91

**Slant
Downcurve, loop
Downcurve,
   undercurve**

Write Away

Ask students to write a sentence about a boy named Eduardo or a girl named Elena. (kinesthetic)

Eduardo and Elena like to dance.

PRACTICE MASTER 49

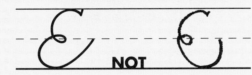

MODEL THE WRITING

Write **E** on guidelines as you say the stroke descriptions. To help students visualize the letter, model **E** in the air. Have students say the stroke descriptions as they write **E** in the air with you. Ask questions such as these:

How many loops are in **E**? *(one)*
Where is it? *(at the midline)*
Where does **E** end? *(at the midline)*

EVALUATE

To help students evaluate their writing, ask questions such as these:
Is the slant of your **E** correct?
Is your loop at the midline?
Are your downcurves the correct size?

PRACTICE

Let students use laminated writing cards or slates to practice writing the letter.

CORRECTIVE STRATEGY

E   *C*

NOT

The bottom downcurve is larger and farther to the left.

Downcurve
Undercurve
Loop, curve right

COACHING HINT

Using card stock or other heavy paper, cut out the parts of a letter (basic strokes) and have the students put them together to form the letter. (kinesthetic)

PRACTICE MASTER 50

Trace and write.
𝒪 𝒪 𝒪 𝒪 𝒪 𝒪 𝒪

Write
Oki Oahu Oman

Ohio is a state

EVALUATE Circle your best.   Circle your best word.
Name

Copyright © Zaner-Bloser, Inc.   PRACTICE MASTER 50

Circle O and 𝒪 in these words.

Our school is in the ocean.

Our school is in the ocean.

Trace and write.
𝒪 𝒪 𝒪 𝒪 𝒪 𝒪

𝒪 is not joined to the letter that follows. Write words that begin with 𝒪.

Otto   October   Ohio

Write a sentence that begins with 𝒪.

Olo saw the ocean.

Circle your best 𝒪.

92

MODEL THE WRITING

Write O on guidelines as you say the stroke descriptions. To help students visualize the letter, model O in the air. Have students say the stroke descriptions as they write O in the air with you. Ask questions such as these:
Where does O begin? (*just below the headline)*
How many pauses are in O? *(none)*

EVALUATE

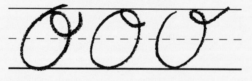

To help students evaluate their writing, ask questions such as these:
Does your O begin below the headline?
Does your O end at the headline?
Is your O closed?

PRACTICE

Let students use laminated writing cards or slates to practice writing the letter.

CORRECTIVE STRATEGY

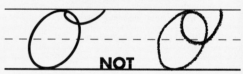

NOT

Dip the loop down slightly, then curve right to end at the headline.

Review

$\mathcal{a}$ $\mathcal{C}$ $\mathcal{E}$ $\mathcal{O}$

Remember!
$\mathcal{a}$, $\mathcal{C}$, and $\mathcal{E}$
are joined to the
letter that follows.

$\mathcal{O}$ is not joined.

Write names of people.

Ellen   Charles   Oki

Alberta   Craig

Circle your
best word.

Write this sentence.

Ed knows Ana.

Is your word
spacing correct?

93

COACHING HINT

Students who hold the pencil too tightly or do not use the correct position may benefit from the use of the Zaner-Bloser Writing Frame. This teaching aid adapts for either right-hand or left-hand use and fosters correct hand position and arm movement. (kinesthetic)

EVALUATE

To help students evaluate their writing, ask questions such as these:
Are your downcurve strokes correct in **A, C, E,** and **O**?
Are your **A, C,** and **E** joined properly to the letter that follows?

REFOCUS

Review the uppercase letters **A, C, E,** and **O** by asking questions such as these: Which letters are joined to the letter that follows? **(A, C, E)** Which letter is not joined to the letter that follows? **(O)**

Ask pairs of students to find four words, one for each of these uppercase letters. Refer them to a class list, nametags, book titles, a glossary, or any other source of words beginning with uppercase letters. Set a time limit of three to five minutes for the search. Ask each pair of students to write their four words on the chalkboard, describing the strokes and joining techniques.

Write **A**way

Ask students to write and illustrate a short story about someone they know whose name begins with **A, C, E,** or **O**. Participate by describing someone you know whose name begins with one of these letters. (kinesthetic)

Alice

**Curve forward, slant
Overcurve, slant
Undercurve**

COACHING HINT

To ensure correct paper placement, place the paper at the proper height on the desk for each student and use tape to create a frame on the desk around each corner of the paper. (Do not tape the paper to the desk.) The student will now be able to place the paper in the correct position. (kinesthetic, visual)

PRACTICE MASTER 51

Circle N and n in these words.

New books are exciting!
new books are exciting!

Trace and write.

| N n | n n n n n |

n is joined to the letter that follows. Write words that begin with n.

November   Nevada

Write a sentence that begins with n.

Circle your best n.

Nya reads a lot.

94

MODEL THE WRITING

Write **N** on guidelines as you say the stroke descriptions. To help students visualize the letter, model **N** in the air. Have students say the stroke descriptions as they write **N** in the air with you. Ask questions such as these:
How does **N** begin? *(with a curve forward)*
How many slant strokes are in **N**? *(two)*

EVALUATE

To help students evaluate their writing, ask questions such as these:
Are your slant strokes pulled toward the baseline?
Is your overcurve round?

PRACTICE

Let students use laminated writing cards or slates to practice writing the letter.

CORRECTIVE STRATEGY

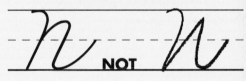

n **NOT** n

Make sure the overcurve is round.

Circle M and *M* in these words.

May we come in?

May we come in?

Trace and write.

M *M*

M M M M M

M is joined to the letter that follows. Write words that begin with *M*.

Monday   Mexico   Ms.

Write a sentence that begins with *M*.

Mo visits Missouri.

Circle your best *M*.

95

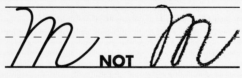

Curve forward, slant
Overcurve, slant
Overcurve, slant
Undercurve

Write Away

I love Mexican music.

PRACTICE MASTER 52

Trace and write.
M M M M M M M

Write.
Milan Munich Mars

My name is May

EVALUATE Circle your best · Circle your best word.
Name

Copyright © Zaner-Bloser, Inc.   PRACTICE MASTER 52

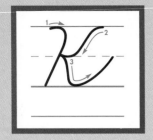

Curve forward, slant,
(lift)
Doublecurve
Curve forward,
undercurve

COACHING HINT

Provide a small amount of shaving cream, a drop of tempera paint, and a paper plate for each student. Direct the students to mix the shaving cream and paint with their fingertips and to practice the strokes and letters you call out. (kinesthetic)

PRACTICE MASTER 53

Circle K and $\mathcal{K}$ in these words.

Keep up the good work!
Keep up the good work!

Trace and write.

K $\mathcal{K}$ $\mathcal{K}$ $\mathcal{K}$ $\mathcal{K}$ $\mathcal{K}$ $\mathcal{K}$

$\mathcal{K}$ is joined to the letter that follows. Write words that begin with $\mathcal{K}$.

Kyoto   Kal   Kansas

Write a sentence that begins with $\mathcal{K}$.

Krista scored a goal.

Circle your best $\mathcal{K}$.

96

MODEL THE WRITING

Write **K** on guidelines as you say the stroke descriptions. To help students visualize the letter, model **K** in the air. Have students say the stroke descriptions as they write **K** in the air with you. Ask questions such as these:
Where is the lift in **K**? *(after the slant)*
What stroke follows the lift? *(doublecurve)*

EVALUATE

To help students evaluate their writing, ask questions such as these:
Does your **K** rest on the baseline?
Is your **K** about the same width as the model?
Does your **K** end at the midline?

PRACTICE

Let students use laminated writing cards or slates to practice writing the letter.

CORRECTIVE STRATEGY

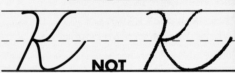

Curve forward before the undercurve ending.

Circle H and *H* in these words.

How old are you?
How old are you?

Trace and write.

H   H   H   H   H

H is joined to the letter that follows. Write words that begin with *H*.

Hungary   Houston

Write a sentence that begins with *H*.

Circle your best *H*.

Hye is eight today.

97

MODEL THE WRITING

Write **H** on guidelines as you say the stroke descriptions. To help students visualize the letter, model **H** in the air. Have students say the stroke descriptions as they write **H** in the air with you. Ask questions such as these:
How many loops are in **H**? *(one)*
How many lifts are in **H**? *(one)*
Where does **H** end? *(at the midline)*

EVALUATE

To help students evaluate their writing, ask questions such as these:
Is your **H** about the same width as the model?
Does your loop touch the first slant stroke at the midline?
Does your **H** end at the midline?

PRACTICE

Let students use laminated writing cards or slates to practice writing the letter.

CORRECTIVE STRATEGY

NOT

Retrace before the loop.

Curve forward, slant, (lift)
Curve back, slant
Retrace, loop, curve right

Write Away

Ask students to make up the name of a country beginning with the letter **H**. Have them write a brief description of their imaginary country. Participate by describing your own imaginary country that begins with the letter **H**. *(kinesthetic)*

Heart Country

PRACTICE MASTER 54

Review the letters **N, M, K,** and **H** by writing them on the chalkboard as students say the strokes with you. Ask questions such as these: Which letters are joined to the letter that follows? *(all)* How do all the letters begin? *(with a curve forward stroke)*

Ask the students whose first, middle, or last names begin with **N, M, K,** and **H** to write their names on the chalkboard.

Write Away

Provide students with a map of the United States. Ask them to write names of states beginning with **N, M, K,** and **H.** Participate by naming a state that begins with one of these letters. *(visual)*

Review

Remember! *n, m, K,* and *H* are joined to the letter that follows.

Write names of states.

Michigan   Kentucky

New Hampshire

Circle your best word.

Write this sentence.

He was in Maine.

Circle a word with correct letter spacing.

98

COACHING HINT: LEFT-HANDED WRITERS

Right-handed teachers can invite a left-handed person to serve as a model. Another teacher, an older student, or a parent could visit the classroom to assist left-handed writers.

EVALUATE

To help students evaluate their writing, ask questions such as these:
Are the size and shape of your **N, M, K,** and **H** satisfactory?
Are **N, M, K,** and **H** joined properly to the letter that follows?

Minnesota

Kansas

North Carolina

Circle U and *U* in these words.

Unicycles are hard to ride.
Unicycles are hard to ride.

Trace and write.

U *U*

U U U U U

U is joined to the letter that follows. Write words that begin with *U*.

Utah   Umeko   Uri

Write a sentence that begins with *U*.

Uncle Uri rides well.

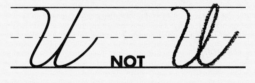

Circle your best *U*

99

Curve forward, slant
Undercurve
Slant, undercurve

Write Away

Ask students to write and illustrate a short description of one of their uncles. Participate by describing one of your uncles. (visual, kinesthetic)

my Uncle Ed

PRACTICE MASTER 55

MODEL THE WRITING

Write **U** on guidelines as you say the stroke descriptions. To help students visualize the letter, model **U** in the air. Have students say the stroke descriptions as they write **U** in the air with you. Ask questions such as these:
How many undercurves are in **U**? *(two)*
Where does the first undercurve end? *(at the headline)*
Where does the second undercurve end? *(at the midline)*

EVALUATE

U U U

To help students evaluate their writing, ask questions such as these:
Are your slant strokes pulled toward the baseline?
Does your first undercurve end at the headline?
Does your **U** rest on the baseline?

PRACTICE

Let students use laminated writing cards or slates to practice writing the letter.

CORRECTIVE STRATEGY

U **NOT** *U*

Pause before the second slant stroke.

**Curve forward, slant
Undercurve
Slant
Loop back, overcurve**

COACHING HINT

Holding the pencil too tightly is a common problem that causes a student to tire easily when writing. To overcome this problem, have the student crumple a piece of paper, place it in the palm of the writing hand, and pick up the pencil. This will serve as a reminder not to squeeze the pencil. (kinesthetic)

PRACTICE MASTER 56

Circle Y and *Y* in these words.

Yo-yos roll up and down.

Yo-yos roll up and down.

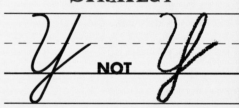

Trace and write.

Y *Y*   *Y Y Y Y Y Y*

Y is joined to the letter that follows. Write words that begin with *Y*.

Yul   Yvette   Yolanda

Write a sentence that begins with *Y*.

You can use my yo-yo.

Circle your best *Y*

MODEL THE WRITING

Write **Y** on guidelines as you say the stroke descriptions. To help students visualize the letter, model **Y** in the air. Have students say the stroke descriptions as they write **Y** in the air with you. Ask questions such as these:
How does **Y** end? *(with an overcurve)*
Where does the loop close? *(at the baseline)*

EVALUATE

Y Y Y

To help students evaluate their writing, ask questions such as these:
Is your **Y** about the same size as the model?
Does your **Y** end with an overcurve?
Does your overcurve cross at the baseline?

PRACTICE

Let students use laminated writing cards or slates to practice writing the letter.

CORRECTIVE STRATEGY

Y **NOT** *Y*

Pause after the undercurve.

Circle Z and *Ȝ* in these words.

Zippers get stuck easily.
Zippers get stuck easily.

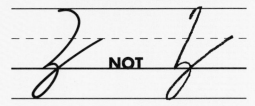

Trace and write.

Z Ȝ   Ȝ   Ȝ   Ȝ   Ȝ   Ȝ

Ȝ is joined to the letter that follows. Write words that begin with *Ȝ*.

Zaire   Zelda   Zach

Write a sentence that begins with *Ȝ*.

Zytka has a red vest.

Circle your best *Ȝ*

101

Curve forward, slant
Overcurve, curve
   down
Loop, overcurve

Write **Away**

Ask students to write and illustrate an advertising slogan for "Zippy Zippers." Participate by telling your own slogan for "Zippy Zippers." (visual, kinesthetic)

Zippy Zippers

are easy to zip!

PRACTICE MASTER 57

MODEL THE WRITING

Write **Z** on guidelines as you say the stroke descriptions. To help students visualize the letter, model **Z** in the air. Have students say the stroke descriptions as they write **Z** in the air with you. Ask questions such as these:

How many loops are in **Z**? *(one)*
How does **Z** end? *(with an overcurve)*

EVALUATE

To help students evaluate their writing, ask questions such as these:
Does your loop fill the descender space?
Are your strokes smooth and even?
Is your **Z** about the same width as the model?

PRACTICE

Let students use laminated writing cards or slates to practice writing the letter.

CORRECTIVE STRATEGY

NOT

Practice writing the curve forward and slant strokes so they flow smoothly into the overcurve at the baseline.

101

Review the letters **U**, **Y**, and **Z** by writing them on the chalkboard as the students say the strokes with you. Ask questions such as these: Which letters are joined to the letter that follows? *(all)* Which letters have a descender? *(Y, Z)* Which letter doesn't have a loop? *(U)*

Write these words on the chalkboard:

United   Yvonne   Zeke

Ask students to do each of the following:
- Write the girl's name three times. Circle the descender. *(Yvonne)*
- Write the boy's name twice. Trace over the uppercase letter. Use a crayon to trace the overcurve stroke that ends the letter. *(Zeke)*
- Write the word that completes the country's name: _____ States. Write the word three times. Trace the undercurve stroke that joins the uppercase letter to the letter that follows. *(United)*

W rite Away

Ask students to choose one of the book titles shown on page 102 and to write a sentence telling why they would like to read that book. Participate by telling which of these books you would like to read and why. (auditory)

Review

Remember! *U, Y,* and *Z* are joined to the letter that follows.

Write the book titles.

Your Kitten and You

Zither Music

Circle your best word.

Write this sentence.

Do *Y* and *Z* go below the baseline?

Uri read Zoos.

102

COACHING HINT

Use a hole punch to cut openings in a large letter made of card stock, construction paper, or other heavy paper and have students use yarn to lace the letter. (kinesthetic, visual)

EVALUATE

To help students evaluate their writing, ask questions such as these:
Which of your joinings are satisfactory?
Which of your joinings need improvement?

Circle V and $\mathcal{V}$ in these words.

Violets are blue.
Violets are blue.

Trace and write.

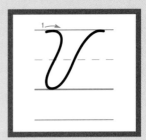

V | V

$\mathcal{V}$ is not joined to the letter that follows. Write words that begin with $\mathcal{V}$.

Virginia   Vermont   Van

Write a sentence that begins with $\mathcal{V}$.

Vicki picks violets.

Circle your best $\mathcal{V}$.

103

**Curve forward, slant
Undercurve
Overcurve**

Ask students to write a sentence about Virginia or Vermont. Participate by telling a fact about one of these states. (kinesthetic)

MODEL THE WRITING

Write **V** on guidelines as you say the stroke descriptions. To help students visualize the letter, model **V** in the air. Have students say the stroke descriptions as they write **V** in the air with you. Ask questions such as these:
How does **V** begin? *(with a curve forward)*
Where does **V** end? *(just below the headline)*

EVALUATE

To help students evaluate their writing, ask questions such as these:
Is your **V** about the same width as the model?
Are the curves in your **V** smooth and even?
Does your **V** end just below the headline?

PRACTICE

Let students use laminated writing cards or slates to practice writing the letter.

CORRECTIVE STRATEGY

$\mathcal{V}$ **NOT** V

Make sure the undercurve is round.

PRACTICE MASTER 58

103

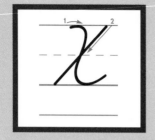

Curve forward, slant,
undercurve, (lift)
Slant

COACHING HINT

Write letters on pieces of
poster board or cardboard
and laminate them. Students
can use them as a base to
form letters with clay.
(kinesthetic, visual)

PRACTICE MASTER 59

Circle X and *X* in these words.

X marks the spot.
X marks the spot.

Trace and write.

X   X   X   X   X   X   X

X is not joined to the letter that follows. Write words that begin with *X*.

X ray   Xenia   Xavier

Write a sentence that begins with *X*.

Xiao used a map.

Circle your best *X*

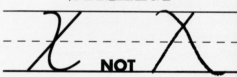

104

MODEL THE WRITING

Write **X** on guidelines as you say the
stroke descriptions. To help students visualize the letter, model **X** in the air. Have
students say the stroke descriptions as they
write **X** in the air with you. Ask questions
such as these:
How does **X** begin? *(with a curve forward)*
Where is the lift? *(after the undercurve)*

EVALUATE

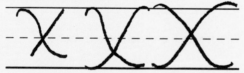

To help students evaluate their writing, ask
questions such as these:
Does your **X** rest on the baseline?
Do your slant strokes cross at the midline?
Is your **X** about the same width as the
model?

PRACTICE

Let students use laminated writing cards or
slates to practice writing the letter.

CORRECTIVE STRATEGY

X   X
         NOT

The second slant stroke crosses the first at
the midline.

Circle W and *W* in these words.

We won the race!
We won the race!

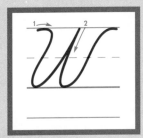

Trace and write.

W is not joined to the letter that follows. Write words that begin with W.

Wednesday   *Wyoming*

Write a sentence that begins with *W*.

Who will race next?

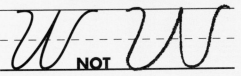

Circle your best *W*.

MODEL THE WRITING

Write **W** on guidelines as you say the stroke descriptions. To help students visualize the letter, model **W** in the air. Have students say the stroke descriptions as they write **W** in the air with you. Ask questions such as these:
Where does **W** begin? (*just below the headline)*
How many undercurves are in **W**? *(two)*

EVALUATE

To help students evaluate their writing, ask questions such as these:
Is your **W** about the same width as the model?
Does your **W** touch the headline three times?

PRACTICE

Let students use laminated writing cards or slates to practice writing the letter.

CORRECTIVE STRATEGY

NOT

Say each stroke as you write the letter.

Curve forward, slant
Undercurve, slant
Undercurve
Overcurve

Write **Away**

Ask students to write a question that begins with *Who, What, When, Where,* or *Why.* Participate by asking a question that begins with one of these words. (kinesthetic)

PRACTICE MASTER 60

Trace and write.

Write
Wisconsin Warsaw

Where is Wales?

EVALUATE Circle your best · Circle your best word.

Name

PRACTICE MASTER 60

Review the letters **V**, **X**, and **W** by asking questions such as these:
Which letters are joined to the letter that follows? *(none)*
Which letters begin with a curve forward? *(all)*
Which letters end with an overcurve? *(V, W)*

Write the following on the chalkboard:

> Ms. Voss
> Mrs. Xavier
> Mr. White

Review the use of titles with names. Remind students that a period is needed after each title. Ask volunteers to come to the chalkboard and write the titles and names of teachers or other people they know that begin with **V**, **X**, and **W**.

Write Away

Ask students to write and illustrate a few sentences about a family. The family name should begin with **V**, **X**, or **W**. Participate by describing a family whose name begins with one of these letters. (visual, auditory)

Review

Remember!
V, *X*, and *W* are not joined to the letter that follows.

Write family names.

Van Winkle   Xanthos

Weiss   Xu   Vitale

Circle your best word.

Write this sentence.

We met Mr. Vail.

Circle the word with the best slant.

106

COACHING HINT: LEFT-HANDED WRITERS

Have the students hold their pencils farther back from the point than right-handed writers do. (kinesthetic)

EVALUATE

To help students evaluate their writing, ask questions such as these:
Which of your letters are shaped correctly?
Which of your letters need improvement in their shape?
Which of your letters are the correct size?
Which of your letters need improvement in their size?

Circle T and *T* in these words.

Today is my birthday.

Today is my birthday.

Trace and write.

T T T T T

T is not joined to the letter that follows. Write words that begin with *T*.

Texas   Thursday   Tom

Write a sentence that begins with *T*.

Today is Tuesday.

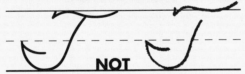

Circle your best *T*.

107

Slant, curve forward
and right, (lift)
Doublecurve,
curve up
Retrace, curve right

Ask students to write a sentence that begins with the word *Today*. Participate by telling something about today. (kinesthetic)

MODEL THE WRITING

Write **T** on guidelines as you say the stroke descriptions. To help students visualize the letter, model **T** in the air. Have students say the stroke descriptions as they write **T** in the air with you. Ask questions such as these:
Where does **T** begin? *(at the headline)*
What is the first stroke in **T**? *(slant)*
Where does **T** end? *(below the midline)*

EVALUATE

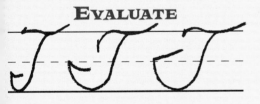

To help students evaluate their writing, ask questions such as these:
Is your **T** about the same width as the model?
Does your **T** begin at the headline?
Does your last stroke curve right?

PRACTICE

Let students use laminated writing cards or slates to practice writing the letter.

CORRECTIVE STRATEGY

NOT

Do not leave space between the top and the body of the letter.

PRACTICE MASTER 61

Trace and write.
T T T T T
Write.
Thailand Tokyo
Tibet is cold.

Slant, curve forward
and right, (lift)
Doublecurve,
curve up
Retrace, curve right,
(lift)
Slide right

COACHING HINT

Students who hold the pencil too tightly or do not use the correct position may benefit from the use of the Zaner-Bloser Writing Frame. This teaching aid adapts for either right-hand or left-hand use and fosters correct hand position and arm movement. (kinesthetic)

PRACTICE MASTER 62

Trace and write.
$\mathcal{F}$ $\mathcal{F}$ $\mathcal{F}$ $\mathcal{F}$ $\mathcal{F}$

Write.
Florence Franco

Faye likes Fiji

EVALUATE Circle your best. Circle your best word.

Name

Copyright © Zaner-Bloser, Inc.   PRACTICE MASTER 62

108

Circle F and $\mathcal{F}$ in these words.

Friends make me smile.
Friends make me smile.

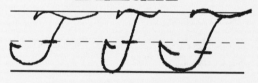

Trace and write.
$\mathcal{F}$ $\mathcal{F}$ $\mathcal{F}$ $\mathcal{F}$ $\mathcal{F}$

$\mathcal{F}$ is not joined to the letter that follows. Write words that begin with $\mathcal{F}$.
Friday Florida Fay

Write a sentence that begins with $\mathcal{F}$.
Fred is a friend.

Circle your best $\mathcal{F}$.

108

MODEL THE WRITING

Write **F** on guidelines as you say the stroke descriptions. To help students visualize the letter, model **F** in the air. Have students say the stroke descriptions as they write **F** in the air with you. Ask questions such as these: How are **T** and **F** alike? *(There is a T in F.)* How are they different? *(In F, the last stroke is a slide right.)*

EVALUATE

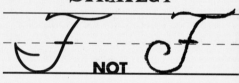

To help students evaluate their writing, ask questions such as these:
Does your **F** rest on the baseline?
Is your **F** about the same width as the model?
Is your slide right stroke at the midline?

PRACTICE

Let students use laminated writing cards or slates to practice writing the letter.

CORRECTIVE STRATEGY

$\mathcal{F}$ NOT $\mathcal{F}$

Pause before the retrace.

Circle I and *I* in these words.

It's snowing!
It's snowing!

Trace and write.

I   I   I   I   I

I is not joined to the letter that follows. Write words that begin with *I*.

Iowa   Idaho   Inacio

Write a sentence that begins with *I*.

I wear snow boots.

Circle your best *I*.

109

Overcurve
Curve down and up
Retrace, curve right

MODEL THE WRITING

Write **I** on guidelines as you say the stroke descriptions. To help students visualize the letter, model **I** in the air. Have students say the stroke descriptions as they write **I** in the air with you. Ask questions such as these:
Where does **I** begin? (*just below the baseline*)
Where is the pause in **I**? (*at the midline before the retrace*)

EVALUATE

To help students evaluate their writing, ask questions such as these:
Does your **I** begin just below the baseline?
Is the slant of your **I** correct?
Is your **I** about the same size as the model?

PRACTICE

Let students use laminated writing cards or slates to practice writing the letter.

CORRECTIVE STRATEGY

I   **NOT**   *I*

Pause after the curve at the midline and retrace.

Write Away

Ask students to write and illustrate a short story telling what they would like to be when they grow up. Participate by telling why you became a teacher. (visual, kinesthetic)

PRACTICE MASTER 63

Trace and write
I   I   I   I   I   I   I   I

Write
Iroquois   Iceland
I'm from Idaho.

EVALUATE Circle your best — Circle your best word

Name

Copyright © Zaner-Bloser, Inc.   PRACTICE MASTER 63

Overcurve
Slant
Loop back, overcurve

COACHING HINT

Have students use a pencil with #2 or softer lead. Make sure students do not apply a lot of pressure to their pencils as they write. (kinesthetic)

PRACTICE MASTER 64

Trace and write.
ℐ ℐ ℐ ℐ ℐ ℐ ℐ ℐ ℐ
Write
Juneau Jamaica
Jupiter is huge
EVALUATE Circle your best ℐ . Circle your best word
Name

Circle J and *ℐ* in these words.

Juggling is not easy.
Juggling is not easy.

Trace and write.

J *ℐ*   *ℐ ℐ ℐ ℐ ℐ*

ℐ is joined to the letter that follows. Write words that begin with *ℐ*.

June   January   July

Write a sentence that begins with *ℐ*.

Juana can juggle.

Circle your best *ℐ*.

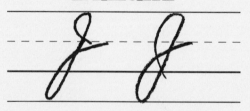

110

MODEL THE WRITING

Write **J** on guidelines as you say the stroke descriptions. To help students visualize the letter, model **J** in the air. Have students say the stroke descriptions as they write **J** in the air with you. Ask questions such as these:
Where does **J** begin? *(just below the baseline)*
Where do the two loops close? *(at the baseline)*
How does **J** begin? *(with an overcurve)*
How does **J** end? *(with an overcurve)*

EVALUATE

ℐ   ℐ

To help students evaluate their writing, ask questions such as these:
Does your **J** begin just below the baseline?
Do your loops close at the baseline?

PRACTICE

Let students use laminated writing cards or slates to practice writing the letter.

CORRECTIVE STRATEGY

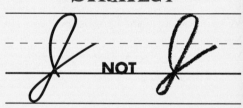

ℐ **NOT** *ℐ*

Make sure the descender fills the space.

Circle Q and *Q* in these words.

Quick! Hide here.

Quick! Hide here.

Trace and write.

Q Q Q Q Q

Q is not joined to the letter that follows. Write words that begin with Q.

Quebec   Querida   Quito

Write a sentence that begins with Q.

Quin hides quietly.

Circle your best *Q*.

III

Curve back,
overcurve
Curve down, retrace
Curve forward, curve
under

Ask students to write and illustrate *Quiet!* followed by a related sentence, as shown on page III with *Quick!* Participate by saying *Quiet!* and your own related sentence. (auditory)

MODEL THE WRITING

Write **Q** on guidelines as you say the stroke descriptions. To help students visualize the letter, model **Q** in the air. Have students say the stroke descriptions as they write **Q** in the air with you. Ask questions such as these:
Where does **Q** begin? *(at the baseline)*
Where does **Q** end? *(just below the baseline)*

EVALUATE

To help students evaluate their writing, ask questions such as these:
Does your **Q** begin at the baseline?
Is your **Q** closed?
Is your **Q** about the same width as the model?

PRACTICE

Let students use laminated writing cards or slates to practice writing the letter.

CORRECTIVE STRATEGY

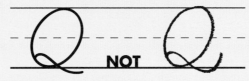

NOT

The curve under stroke ends below the baseline.

PRACTICE MASTER 65

Trace and write
Q Q Q Q Q Q Q

Write
Quaker Qatar

Quincy is nine.

EVALUATE Circle your best ... Circle your best word
Name
Copyright © Zaner-Bloser, Inc.   PRACTICE MASTER 65

111

Review the letters **T, F, I, J,** and **Q** by writing them on the chalkboard as the students say the strokes with you. Ask questions such as these:
Which letter is joined to the letter that follows? *(J)*
Which letters are not joined to the letter that follows? *(T, F, I, Q)*
Which letters begin at the headline? *(T, F)*
Which letters begin below the baseline? *(I, J)*
Which letter ends below the baseline? *(Q)*

Ask five volunteers to come to the chalkboard. Have them write one of the following uppercase letters: **T, F, I, J, Q.** Have each volunteer demonstrate the formation of the letter, then answer the following questions:
• Where does your letter begin?
• Where does your letter end?
• Does your letter have a descender?
• Does your letter join to the letter that follows?

Write Away

Ask students to make up the name of a king or a queen whose name starts with **T, F, I, J,** or **Q.** Have students write and illustrate a short story about a day in the life of their imaginary ruler. (visual, kinesthetic)

King Tall

Review

Remember! *J* is joined to the letter that follows. *T, F, I,* and *Q* are not joined.

Write names of kings and queens.

Frederick   Theresa

John   Isabella

Circle your best word.

Write this sentence.

I saw Queen Tzu.

Circle the word with the best size and shape.

112

COACHING HINT

Tell students they can increase their handwriting speed by eliminating excessive loops and flourishes from their writing. (visual)

EVALUATE

To help students evaluate their writing, ask questions such as these:
Which of your letters are satisfactory?
Which of your letters need improvement?

Circle G and *G* in these words.

Guess how many!
Guess how many!

Trace and write.

G *G* *G* *G* *G*

G is not joined to the letter that follows. Write words that begin with *G*.

German   Gail   Greta

Write a sentence that begins with *G*.

Gus will guess.

Circle your best *G*.

Guess the Number of Marbles

113

Undercurve, loop,
  curve forward
Doublecurve,
  curve up
Retrace, curve right

Write **Away**

Write the following chart on the chalkboard. Ask students to write and complete it. Participate by telling your guess for the first item. (visual, kinesthetic)

HOW MANY?

Objects	Guess	Actual
paper clips in a handful		
crayons in a box		
books on a shelf		

MODEL THE WRITING

Write **G** on guidelines as you say the stroke descriptions. To help students visualize the letter, model **G** in the air. Have students say the stroke descriptions as they write **G** in the air with you. Ask questions such as these:
Where does **G** begin? *(at the baseline)*
Where does the retrace begin? *(at the midline)*

EVALUATE

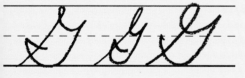

To help students evaluate their writing, ask questions such as these:
Is your loop written from midline to headline?
Is your **G** about the same width as the model?
Does your curve right stroke touch the midline and extend through the undercurve?

PRACTICE

Let students use laminated writing cards or slates to practice writing the letter.

CORRECTIVE STRATEGY

NOT

Pause before the retrace.

PRACTICE MASTER 66

Trace and write.

Write

Grace Gail Gobi

Giorgos is Greek

EVALUATE Circle your best Circle your best word

Name

113

**Undercurve, loop
Curve down and up
Retrace, curve right**

COACHING HINT

Slates are great for letter practice. After you have modeled a letter, ask students to write on their slates before they write in their books or on paper.

Circle S and *S* in these words.

Slide into the water.

Slide into the water.

Trace and write.

| S *S* | *S* *S* *S* *S* *S* |

S is not joined to the letter that follows. Write words that begin with *S*.

Sunday   Saturday

Write a sentence that begins with *S*.

Splash! I'm wet.

Circle your best *S*.

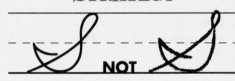

114

MODEL THE WRITING

Write **S** on guidelines as you say the stroke descriptions. To help students visualize the letter, model **S** in the air. Have students say the stroke descriptions as they write **S** in the air with you. Ask questions such as these:
Where does **S** begin? *(at the baseline)*
How many undercurves are in **S**? *(one)*
How many loops are in **S**? *(one)*

EVALUATE

To help students evaluate their writing, ask questions such as these:
Does your **S** have correct slant?
Is the bottom larger than the top?
Does your curve down and up stroke touch the midline?

PRACTICE

Let students use laminated writing cards or slates to practice writing the letter.

CORRECTIVE STRATEGY

NOT

Close the loop at the midline.

114

Circle L and *L* in these words.

Let's fly kites.
Let's fly kites.

Trace and write.

L   L   L   L

L is not joined to the letter that follows. Write words that begin with *L*.

Lou   Luis   Lakeisha

Write a sentence that begins with *L*.

Look at the clouds.

Circle your best *L*.

115

**Undercurve
Loop, curve down
Loop, curve under**

Write **Awa**y

Ask students to make up the name of an imaginary rock star whose initials are **LL**. Have them write and illustrate a brief biography of their imaginary star. Participate by describing your own imaginary rock star with the initials **LL**. (visual, kinesthetic)

Larry the Lion

PRACTICE MASTER 68

MODEL THE WRITING

Write **L** on guidelines as you say the stroke descriptions. To help students visualize the letter, model **L** in the air. Have students say the stroke descriptions as they write **L** in the air with you. Ask questions such as these:
How many loops are in **L**? *(two)*
Where does **L** begin? *(at the midline)*
Where does **L** end? *(just below the baseline)*

EVALUATE

To help students evaluate their writing, ask questions such as these:
Does your **L** begin at the midline?
Does your **L** end just below the baseline?

PRACTICE

Let students use laminated writing cards or slates to practice writing the letter.

CORRECTIVE STRATEGY

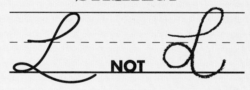

NOT

The lower loop is horizontal and rests on the baseline.

**Doublecurve
Loop, curve down
and up
Loop, curve right**

COACHING HINT

As students near the completion of their handwriting texts, make them aware of their improvement. Comparing students' current writing with samples from the beginning of the year provides motivation for further progress, particularly for students who have had difficulties with handwriting. (visual)

PRACTICE MASTER 69

Circle D and 𝒟 in these words.

Dodge the ball.
Dodge the ball.

Trace and write.

𝒟 is not joined to the letter that follows. Write words that begin with 𝒟.

December   David   Di

Write a sentence that begins with 𝒟.

Did you get hit?

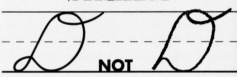

Circle your best 𝒟.

116

MODEL THE WRITING

Write **D** on guidelines as you say the stroke descriptions. Model **D** in the air. Have students say the stroke descriptions as they write **D** in the air with you. Ask questions such as these:
How many loops are in **D**? *(two)*
How many times does **D** touch the baseline? *(two)*
Where does **D** begin? *(at the headline)*

EVALUATE

To help students evaluate their writing, ask questions such as these:
Does your **D** touch the baseline two times?
Is your **D** closed?
Does your **D** end at the headline?

PRACTICE

Let students use laminated writing cards or slates to practice writing the letter.

CORRECTIVE STRATEGY

NOT

Practice the doublecurve stroke that begins **D** and then "rest" the loop on the baseline.

116

Review

Remember! G, S, L, and D are not joined to the letter that follows.

Write these holidays.

Labor Day   *Flag Day*

Write these sentences.

Circle your best word.

Li likes Saturday.

Guy likes Sunday.

Is your word spacing correct?

117

REFOCUS

Write the letters **G**, **S**, **L**, and **D** on the chalkboard. Ask students to name the strokes as you form the letters. Ask questions such as these:
Which letters are joined to the letter that follows? *(none)*
Which letters begin with an undercurve? *(G, S, L)*
Which letter does not end with a curve right? *(L)*

Write the following names on the chalkboard in manuscript. Have students write each name twice in cursive.

    Dave Lewis
    Gail Sanders
    Sari Dennis
    Leandro Gamon

COACHING HINT

The folded-paper technique provides a quick check of letter formation. After students have written the letter three times on practice paper, have them fold the paper back and under, just above the letters written. By placing the paper directly below the model in the book, students can easily compare their letters with the model to determine likenesses and differences. (kinesthetic, visual)

EVALUATE

To help students evaluate their writing, ask questions such as these:
Which of your letters are satisfactory?
Which of your letters need improvement?

Write Away

Ask students to write and illustrate a journal entry describing their activities last Saturday and Sunday. Participate by describing something you did last weekend. (visual, auditory)

Undercurve, slant
Retrace, curve
forward and back

COACHING HINT

Give each student a card on which one of the basic strokes is written. Tell the students to write that basic stroke on paper and to write all the uppercase and lower-case letters that have that basic stroke. (kinesthetic, visual)

PRACTICE MASTER 70

Circle P and $\mathcal{P}$ in these words.

Please sit down.
Please sit down.

P   *P*

Trace and write.

P P P P P

$\mathcal{P}$ is not joined to the letter that follows. Write words that begin with $\mathcal{P}$.

Phil Pam Pedro

Write a sentence that begins with $\mathcal{P}$.

Circle your best $\mathcal{P}$.

Pizza pans are round.

118

MODEL THE WRITING

Write **P** on guidelines as you say the stroke descriptions. To help students visualize the letter, model **P** in the air. Have students say the stroke descriptions as they write **P** in the air with you. Ask questions such as these:
Where does **P** begin? *(at the midline)*
How does **P** begin? *(with an undercurve)*
Where is the retrace? *(at the bottom of the slant stroke)*

EVALUATE

P P P

To help students evaluate their writing, ask questions such as these:
Does your **P** begin at the midline?
Is your **P** about the same width as the model?
Is your **P** closed?

PRACTICE

Let students use laminated writing cards or slates to practice writing the letters.

CORRECTIVE STRATEGY

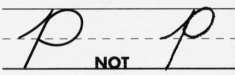

NOT

The forward oval curves around and goes below the midline.

Circle R and *R* in these words.

Rain, rain, go away!
Rain, rain, go away!

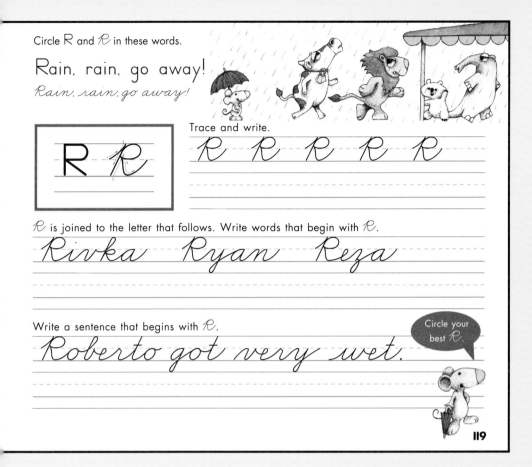

Trace and write.

R R R R R

R is joined to the letter that follows. Write words that begin with *R*.

Rivka   Ryan   Reza

Write a sentence that begins with *R*.

Roberto got very wet.

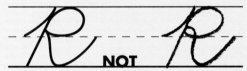

Circle your best *R*.

119

Write Away

Ask students to write a poem about rain. Participate by sharing a poem about rain. (kinesthetic)

MODEL THE WRITING

Write **R** on guidelines as you say the stroke descriptions. To help students visualize the letter, model **R** in the air. Have students say the stroke descriptions as they write **R** in the air with you. Ask questions such as these:
Where does **R** end? *(at the midline)*
What is the ending stroke? *(undercurve)*

EVALUATE

To help students evaluate their writing, ask questions such as these:
Does your **R** begin at the midline?
Does your **R** end at the midline?
Does your retrace look like a single line?

PRACTICE

Let students use laminated writing cards or slates to practice writing the letter.

CORRECTIVE STRATEGY

R **NOT** *R*

Pause at the slant stroke before beginning the second curve forward.

PRACTICE MASTER 71

Trace and write.
R R R R R R

Write:
Richmond Ryan

Ray likes Rome

EVALUATE Circle your best · Circle your best word
Name

Copyright © Zaner-Bloser, Inc.   **PRACTICE MASTER 71**

119

**Undercurve, slant
Retrace, curve
  forward, loop
Curve forward and
  back
Retrace, curve right**

COACHING HINT

On the chalkboard, write a line of uppercase letters with several obvious errors. Ask students to come to the chalkboard to locate, identify, and correct the errors. (visual, kinesthetic)

PRACTICE MASTER 72

Trace and write
𝓑 𝓑 𝓑 𝓑 𝓑 𝓑 𝓑 𝓑

Write
Bette Bonn Bali

Bermuda is warm

EVALUATE Circle your best   Circle your best word

Name

Copyright © Zaner-Bloser, Inc.   PRACTICE MASTER 72

Circle B and 𝓑 in these words.

Basketball is fun to play.
Basketball is fun to play.

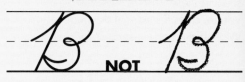

Trace and write.

B 𝓑   𝓑 𝓑 𝓑 𝓑 𝓑

𝓑 is not joined to the letter that follows. Write words that begin with 𝓑.

Boise Beatriz Brooke

Write a sentence that begins with 𝓑.

Betty is our coach.

Circle your best 𝓑.

MODEL THE WRITING

Write **B** on guidelines as you say the stroke descriptions. To help students visualize the letter, model **B** in the air. Have students say the stroke descriptions as they write **B** in the air with you. Ask questions such as these:
How are **B** and **R** alike? *(They have the same beginning.)*
Where does the loop close? *(at the midline)*
What other letters have the retrace and curve right ending? *(I, G, T, F, S)*

EVALUATE

To help students evaluate their writing, ask questions such as these:
Does your **B** have correct slant?
Is your loop at the midline?
Does your **B** rest on the baseline?

PRACTICE

Let students use laminated writing cards or slates to practice writing the letter.

CORRECTIVE STRATEGY

𝓑 NOT 𝓑

Make sure the ending stroke touches the slant stroke.

Review

Remember! *R* is joined to the letter that follows. *P* and *B* are not joined.

Write names of book characters.

Christopher Robin

Pooh Bear   *Rabbit*

Circle your best word.

Write this sentence.

Piglet likes Roo.

Circle a word with correct letter spacing.

121

COACHING HINT

Place a small amount of shaving cream on each student's desk. Direct students to spread the shaving cream over their desks. Ask them to practice the strokes and letters you call out. Repeat several times and allow time for students to experiment with various patterns of strokes. This is an effective exercise for reinforcing stroke and letter formations and also a good way to clean the desks. (kinesthetic)

EVALUATE

To help students evaluate their writing, ask questions such as these:
Which of your letters are satisfactory?
Which of your letters need improvement?

REFOCUS

Write the letters **P, R,** and **B** on the chalkboard. Say the strokes as you write the letters. Ask questions such as these:
Which letter is joined to the letter that follows? *(R)*
Which letters are not joined to the letter that follows? *(P, B)*
Which letters are made with one forward oval? *(P, R)*
Which letter is made with two forward ovals? *(B)*

Ask a volunteer to face the chalkboard and form these letters in the air with broad, sweeping motions. Ask students to identify the letters.

Write Away

Ask students to write a description of one of the book characters named on page 121. Participate by reading a Winnie-the-Pooh story to the class or by describing the characters in a Winnie-the-Pooh story. (auditory)

Slant

Slant, curve
    forward, slant
Curve right

Slant, curve
    forward and back
Curve forward
    and back

Slant
Slide right, (lift)
Slant

Slant
Curve forward
    and back, (lift)
Slide right

Numerals and Number Words

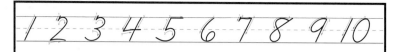

Write numerals.

Fill in the missing numerals on the balloons.

Circle your best numeral.

122

MODEL THE WRITING

Write the numerals on guidelines as you say the stroke descriptions. To help students visualize each numeral, model it in the air. Have students say the stroke descriptions as they write each numeral in the air with you. Ask questions such as these:

Where does the numeral **1** begin? *(at the headline)*

What stroke begins the numerals **2, 3,** and **7**? *(short slant)*

What is the last stroke in the numeral **5**? *(slide right)*

Where does the numeral **8** begin? *(just below the headline)*

PRACTICE MASTER 73

Trace and write.

1 1 2 2 3 3 4 4

5 5 6 6 7 7 8 8

9 9 10 10

EVALUATE Circle your best numeral.

Name

Copyright © Zaner-Bloser, Inc.   PRACTICE MASTER 73

Write number words.

one   two   three   four

five   six   seven

eight   nine   ten

Write the answers in words.

one plus two _____

eight minus two _____

four plus three _____

Circle your best number word.

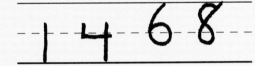

123

COACHING HINT
Provide a shallow tray or box lid with a thin layer of sand in it. Allow students to form their numerals in the sand. (visual, kinesthetic)

EVALUATE

$$1 \; 4 \; 6 \; 8$$

To help students evaluate their writing, ask questions such as these:
Do your numerals touch the headline?
Do your numerals rest on the baseline?

Curve down and forward
Loop

Slant, doublecurve
Slant

Curve back and down
Curve back, slant up

Downcurve, undercurve
Slant

Slant, (lift)
Downcurve, undercurve

Tell students they now have studied and written all the uppercase cursive letter-forms. Guide them in a review of these letters with the following activity.

1. The letters A, C, E, N, M, K, H, U, Y, Z, J, and R are _____ to the letter that follows. (joined)
2. The letters O, V, X, W, T, F, I, Q, G, S, L, D, P, and B are _____ to the letter that follows. (not joined)
3. All uppercase letters are _____ letters. (tall)
4. The uppercase letters with descenders are _____. (*J, Y, Z*)

Have students review and practice the basic cursive strokes.

Review Uppercase Letters

Write these uppercase letters in cursive.

A O C E

H M N K

U Y Z

X W V

F T J Q I

D L G S

B P R

Circle your best letter.

124

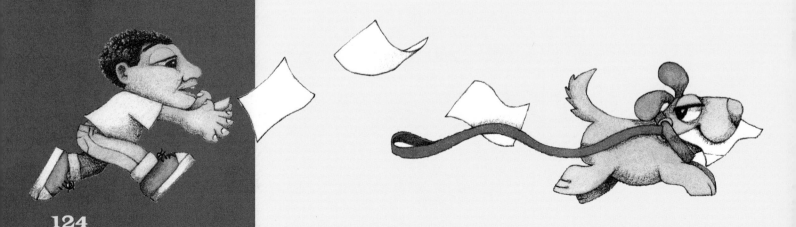

Remember! These letters are joined to the letter that follows

R K H J U A Y C M Z E N

G F O S T X B Q L D P I V W

These letters are not joined.

Write these names in cursive.

Robin Hood

Liberty Bell

Mexico City

World Series

Mount Fuji

Circle your best word.

125

COACHING HINT

Students who have mastered the skill of writing the uppercase and lowercase letters without models should be given writing activities that will challenge them and require thinking.

EVALUATE

To help students evaluate their writing, ask questions such as these:
Which of your letters are satisfactory?
Which of your letters need improvement?
Which of your joinings are satisfactory?
Which of your joinings need improvement?

Write Away

Ask students to describe how learning to write has affected or influenced them. Describe any memories you may have about learning cursive writing. (auditory)

Remind students that at the beginning of the school year they wrote this poem as a pretest and evaluated their handwriting. As they write the poem in cursive, remind them to use correct letter size and shape, uniform slant, and correct spacing. (visual, auditory, kinesthetic)

Posttest

I Can

I can write a story.
I can write a poem.
I can write at school,
And I can write at home.

Write this poem in your best handwriting.
Pay attention to size and shape, slant, and spacing.

Put a star next to your best line of writing.

126

EVALUATE

Have students use the keys to legibility to evaluate their handwriting. Meet individually with students to help them assess their progress.

Certificates of Progress *should be awarded to those students who show notable handwriting progress and* Certificates of Excellence *to those who progress to the top levels of handwriting ability.*

Record of Student's Handwriting Skills

Manuscript/*Cursive*

	Needs Improvement	Shows Mastery		Needs Improvement	Shows Mastery
Positions paper correctly for manuscript writing	☐	☐	Writes downcurve strokes	☐	☐
Holds pencil correctly	☐	☐	Writes overcurve strokes	☐	☐
Writes pull down straight lines	☐	☐	Writes slant strokes	☐	☐
Writes slide right and slide left lines	☐	☐	Writes cursive **i, t, u, w**	☐	☐
Writes backward circles	☐	☐	Writes cursive **r, s, p, j**	☐	☐
Writes forward circles	☐	☐	Writes cursive **a, c, d, q, g, o**	☐	☐
Writes slant lines	☐	☐	Writes cursive **n, m, x, y, z, v**	☐	☐
Writes manuscript **lL, iI, tT**	☐	☐	Writes cursive **e, l, h, k, f, b**	☐	☐
Writes manuscript **oO, aA, dD**	☐	☐	Writes cursive **A, C, E, O**	☐	☐
Writes manuscript **cC, eE, fF**	☐	☐	Writes cursive **N, M, K, H**	☐	☐
Writes manuscript **gG, jJ, qQ**	☐	☐	Writes cursive **U, Y, Z**	☐	☐
Writes manuscript numerals	☐	☐	Writes cursive **V, X, W**	☐	☐
Writes manuscript **uU, sS**	☐	☐	Writes cursive **T, F**	☐	☐
Writes manuscript **bB, pP, rR**	☐	☐	Writes cursive **I, J, Q**	☐	☐
Writes manuscript **nN, mM, hH**	☐	☐	Writes cursive **G, S, L, D**	☐	☐
Writes manuscript **vV, yY, wW**	☐	☐	Writes cursive **P, R, B**	☐	☐
Writes manuscript **xX, kK, zZ**	☐	☐	Writes cursive numerals	☐	☐
Positions paper correctly for cursive writing	☐	☐	Writes with correct size and shape	☐	☐
Writes undercurve strokes	☐	☐	Writes with correct slant	☐	☐
			Writes with correct spacing	☐	☐

127

The Record of Student's Handwriting Skills is reproduced on Practice Master 74.

COACHING HINT

If a student needs improvement, reevaluate his or her writing following practice over a period of time. Invite the student to share in the evaluation.

EVALUATE

The Record of Student's Handwriting Skills serves to indicate each student's progress in mastering the skills presented. The chart lists the essential skills in the program. After the skills that are listed have been practiced and evaluated, you will be able to mark the Record of Student's Handwriting Skills for either *Shows Mastery* or *Needs Improvement*.

Shows Mastery Mastery of written letterforms is achieved when the student writes the letters using correct basic strokes. Compare the student's written letterforms with the letter models shown in the book. Keep in mind the keys to legibility (size and shape, slant, and spacing) when evaluating letters, numerals, punctuation marks, words, and sentences for mastery of skill. Observation will indicate whether a student has mastered such skills as pencil and paper positions.

Needs Improvement If a student has not mastered a skill, provide additional basic instruction and practice. First, determine the student's specific needs. Then return to the initial teaching steps of the lesson for ways to help the student. To improve letterforms, have the student practice writing the letter in isolation and within words and sentences. Reinforce instruction through activities geared to the student's modality strengths. When mastery of the skill is achieved, check Shows Mastery.

Index